Economies of Salvation

Adam Smith and Hegel

Economies of Salvation

Adam Smith and Hegel

Yong-Sun Yang

PETER LANG
Oxford · Bern · Berlin · Bruxelles · Frankfurt am Main · New York · Wien

Bibliographic information published by Die Deutsche Nationalbibliothek
Die Deutsche Nationalbibliothek lists this publication in the Deutsche Nationalbibliografie; detailed bibliographic data is available on the Internet at http://dnb.d-nb.de.

A catalogue record for this book is available from the British Library.

Library of Congress Cataloging-in-Publication Data:

Yang, Yong-Sun.
Economies of salvation : Adam Smith and Hegel / Yong-Sun Yang.
p. cm.
Includes bibliographical references (p.) and index.
ISBN 978-3-0343-0259-3 (alk. paper)
1. Economics--Religious aspects--Christianity. 2. Smith, Adam, 1723-1790. 3. Hegel, Georg Wilhelm Friedrich, 1770-1831. 4. Salvation--Christianity. 5. Self-interest. I. Title.
BR115.E3Y36 2011
261.8'5--dc23
2011040087

ISBN 978-3-0343-0259-3

Cover designed by Gemma Lewis

Printed in Germany

To our children:
Sora, Sori, Haneul, and Jeonghun

Contents

Acknowledgements

I would like to thank my colleagues, students and friends. They have always been the reason for me to continue this worthwhile endeavor. It is also my great pleasure to have a chance to express sincere appreciation to Prof. Paul Oslington, Mr. Graeme McMartin and Dr. Charles Hyde for their knowledge, time and support. This book is dedicated to the memory of my parents, who poured out their lives for their children to live, love and learn the truth and beauty of life. I hope that this is not the end but the beginning of a new journey, with great wonder and joy beyond language and thought.

Abstract

This book challenges the general notion that economics and theology are different academic disciplines. By exploring the relationship between economics and theology through the concept of salvation, this book bridges the gap between the two disciplines and offers a new understanding of their relationship. The meaning and role of self-consciousness in human salvation is developed in relation to major philosophers Adam Smith and G.W.F. Hegel. Smith's self-interest is a natural instinct, while Hegel's self-consciousness is a rational ability. By illuminating the theological foundations of the economic ideas of these two main thinkers, this book enriches our understanding of the issues related to salvation such as: sympathy and recognition, poverty and the state, the invisible hand and the cunning of reason, evil and scarcity, and eschatology. This exploration of their thoughts to clarify the inherent relationship between economics and theology may thus contribute to a better understanding of salvation. The book also provides a model for future dialogue between economists and theologians and extends the frontier of this relatively unexplored field of research.

Abbreviations

EPS	Adam Smith, *Essays on Philosophical Subjects*
PR	G.W.F. Hegel, *Elements of the Philosophy of Right*
TMS	Adam Smith, *The Theory of Moral Sentiments*
WN	Adam Smith, *An Inquiry into the Nature and Causes of the Wealth of Nations*

CHAPTER 1

Introduction: Beginning of Dialogue Between Economics and Theology

1.1. Economics, Ethics, and Theology

This book explores a mutual relationship between economics and theology, which are generally regarded as separate academic disciplines with ethics somewhere in the middle. Economics is usually thought of as a value-free science dealing with facts, while theology is considered to be a value-laden science searching for a spiritual truth. An economic human is assumed to be a rational being looking for the maximization of self-interest, while a religious human is believed to be a self-sacrificing man devoting his life for the benefit of others. Thus, there seems to be a big gap between the views offered by economics and theology in terms of what we want and who we are. These world views are so different from each other that it would seem impossible to establish a dialogue between economics and theology.

Despite the gulf between the assumptions and goals of economics and theology, upon closer inspection it is revealed that there are important linkages between the two disciplines. Indeed, the wide gap between the two disciplines is a relatively recent development and in earlier times economics and theology were much more closely intertwined.[1] Many economic terms and ideas are used in the Bible to explain theological issues such as sins and salvation. The parable about the workers in the vineyard is a good example of an economic image of religious salvation (Matthew 20: 1–16).

1 A.M.C. Waterman, *Revolution, Economics and Religion: Christian Political Economy 1798–1833* (Cambridge: Cambridge University Press, 1991).

The use of economic language to describe religious salvation shows the possibility of establishing a relationship between these seemingly separate subjects.[2]

So what does economics have to do with theology? And what does theology have to do with economics? What is the legitimate relationship between the human economy and God's providence, if any? That is the central question which this book addresses. Nelson argues that economics is fundamentally theology as the seemingly value-free science is actually based on a powerful secular faith in economic progress.[3] However, even though it may be true that economics grounded on fact is actually founded on religious faith of material progressivism, it does not necessarily mean that economics is theology. One possibility is that the relationship between the two disciplines is a matter of ethics rather than of theology or religion itself.[4] For example, Deirdre McCloskey argues in her book *The Bourgeois Virtue* that economics and theology cannot be separated because the bourgeois economic mind has an ethical foundation, promoting a wide range of virtues including typical Christian ethics such as love, faith and hope.[5] However, the hidden interrelationship between economics and theology may reside in more than just an ethical dimension. The aim of this book is to show that the relationship between economics and theology is more than a matter of ethics: economic thought is fundamentally based on theological thought, and religious faith also has a strong economic aspect.

2 Douglas Meeks, *God the Economist: The Doctrine of God in Political Economy* (Minneapolis: Fortress Press, 1990).

3 Robert H. Nelson, 'The Theological Meaning of Economics,' *Christian Century* (August 1993), 777–781. He published two important books: *Reaching for Heaven on Earth – The Theological Meaning of Economics* (1991), *Economics as Religion: from Samuelson to Chicago and Beyond* (2001).

4 Paul Oslington (ed.), *Economics and Religion* (Cheltenham: Edward Elgar 2 volumes, 2003).

5 Deirdre N. McCloskey, *The Bourgeois Virtues: Ethics for an Age of Commerce* (Chicago: University of Chicago Press, 2006).

1.2. Salvation as a Possible Contact Point

In spite of the difficulty of communication between economics and theology today, we cannot deny that a simple reality of human nature is that we have a natural desire for happiness. A human is a self-conscious being who is aware of his own desire for happiness in body, mind, and soul, always searching for economic, moral, and religious satisfaction. It is also undeniable fact that we all have a natural desire for salvation in this world or in a life to come, whatever form that takes. In this book, salvation is chosen as a contact point for economics and theology.

It is interesting to note that salvation has various meanings in both secular and religious circles. In our market-oriented society, people appear to seek salvation primarily, if not entirely, through the attainment of material affluence. Individuals and society seek to be saved from the world of economic scarcity through the maximization of their satisfaction of material consumption. Thus, in economics, self-interest and self-love are seen as the path to salvation. Of course, this belief system does not necessarily mean that material affluence automatically leads us to salvation, nor does it imply that salvation is purely an economic matter. In fact, salvation is not just a matter of having but also a matter of being. In the religious world, self-denial and self-sacrifice (in contrast to self-interest and self-love) are generally considered the way to achieve salvation. Religious salvation is generally believed to be based on others-interest, self-negation, or self-sacrifice by denying ourselves and loving God and others in order to be saved from sin and evil (Matthew 16:24–26). Self-love is by and large regarded as sinful in the religious world.

Religious salvation in connection with sin, self-negation, love, grace, heaven, and eternal life seems to be in fundamental contradiction to the economic salvation which is related to scarce resources, self-interest, competition, rational choice, utility-maximization, and worldly life. In spite of this obvious tension, it is also true that self-consciousness is the essence of the economic and religious desire for salvation in this world or in a world to come. Therefore, salvation is suggested in this book as a contact point to explore the interrelationship between economics and theology.

The self-conscious human desire to achieve ultimate happiness not only in this world but also in any life to come is universal. In this book, the self-conscious human desire for happiness is used as a starting point to explore the relationship between economics and theology with salvation as the key contact point between the two disciplines. Even in religious self-sacrificial behaviour, we may reasonably assume that self-interest is still at the centre of human desire for salvation. Self-sacrifice is possible and meaningful only when we know what self-interest is; self-interest has no meaning at all without others-interest as self-interest is essentially relational rather than solipsistic. The intertwinement of self-interest and others-interest will be one of the important keys with which to understand the human self-conscious desire for salvation.

Human self-consciousness is like a prism which shows various colours depending on which perspective we adopt. It has so broad a range of meanings that it is sometimes problematic. These various colours of self-interest sometimes become the reasons why there are difficulties and misunderstandings in dialogues between economic theory and religious belief. Self-interest as the human desire to better one's condition in terms of happiness is quite often identified with, and criticised as, selfishness, a blind self-autonomy, and distorted self-love in opposition to others-interest, social welfare, and God-love. According to these critiques, self-interest is nothing but economic irrationality, moral depravity, and religious sin. In this book, however, self-interest is more broadly identified with a whole range of colours emerging from the prism of human self-consciousness. This book shows that different approaches to understanding the role of self-interest in achieving salvation do not just give rise to different expressions of the same idea, but rather have different theological assumptions embedded in them. It is also shown that self-interest and others-interest are two faces of the same human self-consciousness.

1.3. Why Adam Smith and G.W.F. Hegel?

There have been many scholarly debates over the issue of the relationship between economics and religion. However, the approach taken in the book is neither an ethical and theological evaluation of economic behaviour in the market, nor an economic analysis of religious behaviour, nor an historical examination of their original relationship, but an exploration of the common base on which they may communicate with each other. In order to demonstrate the full extent of the common ground shared by economics and religion, we need to give a balanced account of both the economic ideas and the theological thought.

This book focuses on the ideas developed by Adam Smith and G.W.F. Hegel. Not only have they both had a huge influence on our way of thought, but they are also quite different thinkers to each other in many respects. Adam Smith is hailed as the father of modern economics, while Hegel is one of the most influential thinkers in philosophy and theology. However, little research has been done so far to directly compare Adam Smith and Hegel especially from the perspective of the interrelationship between economics and theology. The exploration of their thoughts to clarify the inherent relationship between economics and theology may contribute to the extension of the frontier of this unexplored field of research.

Adam Smith as a moral philosopher does not neglect the importance of the moral dimension in human relationships. He believes that humans are born into society not as solipsistic atoms but as relational persons, so that the society we live in is more than just a simple sum of individuals. His idea of self-interest is not selfishness but rather natural self-consciousness of the need to harmonize the tension between individual desire and social welfare. It is therefore important to understand the economic, moral and theological reasons for why he pays so much attention to the role of self-interest as the driver of benefit for both individuals and society.

In addition, his idea of the invisible hand is still a problematic concept perplexing many modern economists as there is certainly a theological flavour in his use of the term. Is there any hidden theological presumption when he refers to the invisible hand, or is it just an ironic joke? What is his understanding of the role of God's providence for human salvation individually and socially? What theological precepts are embedded in his economic ideas? These are the questions to be discussed in Adam Smith's theology of economic life.

The other thinker to be dealt with in this book is G.W.F. Hegel. He is well-known for the circular and dialectical logic which pervades his system of thought. While he is surely not an economist in a modern sense, his direct or indirect influence on modern economics cannot be neglected. In particular, close attention needs to be paid to his idea of the "cunning of reason" because its recognition of the positive role of human passion in history seems to be peculiar considering his strong emphasis on human rational ability. What does he try to convey by the expression "the cunning of reason"? Is there any theological basis for asserting that human passion is the cunning of reason? How does he bring in original sin to his system of thought? What are the theological precepts embedded in his economic ideas? If there are any, how do the theological backgrounds affect his economic ideas? What do those conclusions imply regarding the relationship between economics and theology? And, finally, what is the meaning of salvation in Hegel's theology of economic life? These are the main questions to be discussed.

Of course, it is not easy to compare two great thinkers who have completely different intellectual backgrounds, let alone their different languages and cultures. However, this interdisciplinary comparison will bear fruitful implications if we are able to identify the common base on which these two thinkers have built their ideas. This book shows that the comparison between Adam Smith and Hegel is not only possible, but is also meaningful and enriches our understanding of salvation.

1.4. Aim of the Book

The aim of this interdisciplinary book is to show that economics and theology are mutually intertwined, and that understanding these links contributes to a better understanding of human behaviour not only in the economic world but also in the ethical and religious world. The book will explore the theological dimensions of self-interest, the intertwinement of economics and theology, and its implications for the meaning of salvation.

The first task is to show that human behaviour based on self-interest has a theological dimension. This book will explain that human self-conscious desire is a common foundation on which economics and theology can stand together, and that this desire is the basis of salvation in the thinking of both Adam Smith and Hegel. It will be shown that self-interest as human self-conscious desire is neither moral depravity against community nor religious sin against God, but a way of salvation for individuals and society in this world or in a world to come.

The second task is to show that there is an interrelationship between economics and theology. It will be shown that economic thought has a theological foundation, and that theology has an economic aspect. Different theologies lead to different economic thoughts, and theological investigation of human behaviour cannot avoid economics and its account of human self-conscious desire as a way of salvation.

The third task is to clarify the meaning of salvation in the theologies of economics of Adam Smith and Hegel. It will be shown that salvation is not an issue to be understood exclusively by either economics or theology, but an issue to be dealt with by an interdisciplinary approach as it has economic, moral and theological dimensions. By investigating the role of God's providence in human self-conscious desire, the issues of theodicy and eschatology will be examined to clarify the meaning of salvation of Adam Smith and Hegel.

This book will conclude that human self-conscious desire has economic, moral, and theological dimensions, and it is a way of salvation not only in economics but also in theology. Economics and theology are not separate but mutually interrelated in the theologies of economics of Adam Smith and Hegel. Faith is a kind of self-conscious desire for salvation.

1.5. Structure of the Book

In this section, a brief overview of each chapter is given. The first two chapters are devoted to examining the theology of economic life in Adam Smith and Hegel as preparation for further discussions in the following chapters. Chapter 2 looks at the theological structure of Adam Smith's economic thought. Its aim is to show that economic ideas have theological foundations in his system of thought. Classifying the various arguments in regard to the role of self-interest and pointing out their weakness, it will be argued that self-interest is a way of salvation in Adam Smith's theology of economics. It concludes that economics is interrelated with theology. Chapter 3 examines the theological backgrounds of Hegel's economic ideas. Its purpose is to show that economics and theology cannot be separate in Hegel's theology of economics. By analyzing his approach to original sin, it will be argued that human self-conscious desire is a way of salvation in his theology of economics. It will conclude that there is an interrelationship between economic ideas and theological thought.

Building on Chapters 2 and 3, Chapter 4 looks closely at how Adam Smith and Hegel use human self-conscious desire to explain human behaviour. The aim of the chapter is to show that Adam Smith's sympathy and Hegel's recognition (*Anerkennung*) are based on human self-conscious desire in their theology of economic life. By pointing out that sympathy is natural for Adam Smith and rational (*vernunftig*) for Hegel, it will be argued that the bifurcation comes from the differences in their theological backgrounds. The chapter pays particular attention to the dialectical aspects of human self-conscious desire.

In Chapter 5, Adam Smith's invisible hand is compared with Hegel's cunning of reason. Every theory has its own limits, and those of Adam Smith and Hegel are no exception. The aim of the chapter is to show that two seemingly different ideas are actually consistent and fit their respective theologies of economics. Adam Smith's invisible hand and Hegel's cunning of reason offer a window through which to see the theological landscape in their thoughts. By emphasizing the theological dimension of human self-conscious desire, it will be argued that, far from being unnecessary or ironic constructs or providing an escape from human responsibility,

Adam Smith's invisible hand and Hegel's cunning of reason are expressions of God's providence in their theology of economic life. Further, it argues that there is consistency in Adam Smith's use of the invisible hand in his works. Chapter 5 contributes to the aim of the book by showing that God's providence is the essential concept without which human behaviour cannot properly be understood in Adam Smith and Hegel's theology of economics.

Chapter 6 looks at the matter of economic poverty and the role of the state by examining the theological reasons why Adam Smith and Hegel take different approaches to the problem. Poverty is a universal problem in our society, afflicting both advanced and developing countries. In this economically baptised society, happiness is believed to depend on economic wealth and power; so poverty is identified with the absence of happiness. The scope of the intervention of the state to solve the matter of poverty is an important issue in modern economics. Interestingly, the two thinkers stand on opposite sides in regards to the role of the state and the meaning of poverty. It will be argued that Adam Smith sees poverty as natural, so the intervention of the state is undesirable in his theology of economic life, while Hegel sees poverty as irrational and so it is required that the state should seek to solve this problem. This chapter will show that the economic phenomenon of poverty and the associated role of the state are fundamentally theological issues in the context of the theologies of economics of both Adam Smith and Hegel.

Chapter 7 looks at the issue of evil and the goodness of God. If God is good and all-mighty, where does evil come from? Theodicy is the branch of theology that tries to understand how it can be that God is good and all-powerful in spite of the reality of evil in the world. The aim of Chapter 7 is to investigate the meaning of evil and the way of God's dealing with it in Adam Smith and Hegel's theology of economics. By emphasizing the theological assumptions embedded in their economic ideas, this chapter will show that in Adam Smith's theology of economics self-conscious desire is not sin, and economic scarcity is not evil while, in contrast, Hegel believes that self-interest is related to sin and economic scarcity is an evil that should be overcome by the development of human self-consciousness. This chapter shows that economic ideas regarding self-conscious desire and material scarcity have theological foundations in concepts such as sin and evil.

The issue of theodicy of the present world in chapter 7 leads naturally to a discussion of possible future worlds. The topic of eschatology is dealt with in chapter 8 before a discussion of salvation in chapter 9. Chapter 8 contrasts the eschatological aspects of the theology of economics of Adam Smith and Hegel. By examining the theological structures embedded in their economic thoughts, it will be shown that there is a clear difference between their eschatological approaches to issues such as the afterlife and the kingdom of God. This chapter illustrates that the theological issue of eschatology is closely related to economic ideas.

Chapter 9 looks at the issue of salvation by comparing Adam Smith's notion of salvation with that of Hegel. By drawing upon all of the arguments in the preceding chapters, it will be shown that salvation is a matter of the triadic relationship of the self with interests, others, and God, and involves economic, moral and theological dimensions. This chapter is followed by the conclusion in chapter 10.

CHAPTER 2

Adam Smith's Self-interest as a Way of Salvation

There has been a long-running scholarly debate over the nature of Adam Smith's notion of self-interest. Self-interest is a concept that is fundamental to an understanding of human salvation in economics and theology, though it is easily confused with moral depravity and the consequence of the Fall of humanity. The aim of this chapter is to clarify the meaning and role of self-interest in Adam Smith's theology of economic life. What does he mean by self-interest? What is its role for salvation? What kind of theology might be embedded in his economic ideas, if any? This chapter answers these questions and builds on the discussion in following chapters.

One's interpretation of Adam Smith's notion of self-interest depends very much on the perspective adopted. Calm passion[1] and the soul of the modern human[2] are two examples of positive interpretations of the meaning and role of self-interest. However, there is also criticism coming from people who adopt other perspectives such as that self-interest is based on human depravity against virtue[3] and grace,[4] to name a few. In these various approaches, there is a fundamental tension between secular reason and religious faith.

This chapter takes a different approach from previous research as the theological dimension of self-interest seems to be simplified, neglected or

1 Albert Hirschman, *The Passions and the Interests: Political Arguments for Capitalism before Its Triumph* (Princeton, NJ: Princeton University Press, 1977).

2 Milton Myers, *The Soul of Modern Economic Man: Ideas of Self-Interest, Thomas Hobbes to Adam Smith* (Chicago: University of Chicago Press, 1983).

3 Alasdair MacIntyre, *After Virtue – A Study in Moral Theory* (London: Duckworth, 1981).

4 John Milbank, *Theology and Social Theory: Beyond Secular Reason* (Oxford: Basil Blackwell, 1990).

even denied in those approaches. By identifying nature and providence as the two main poles for Adam Smith's self-interest, it will be shown that his self-interest has economic, moral, and theological dimensions. This chapter will conclude that in Adam Smith's theology of economics, self-interest is neither sin nor culpability but a way of salvation as it is an innate instinct embedded in human nature by God's providence..

2.1. Two Poles of Adam Smith's Self-interest: Nature and Providence

Self-interest is one of the most widely discussed but most misunderstood concepts, not only in daily life but also in academic discussions of economics and theology. In modern economics, a human is assumed to be an economic being who has a single-minded pursuit of self-interest. Self-interest is then nothing but an economic rationality. However, this conception of self-interest is often criticised as implying moral depravity and a lack of ethical awareness. Furthermore, it is sometimes regarded in Christian theology as a vice that is characteristic of the Fall of Man. These various critiques are valid in the sense that the depiction above does not fully capture the full meaning of self-interest. The purpose of this section is to show that Adam Smith's self-interest is a human self-conscious desire more than a calculative rationality, moral depravity, or the consequence of the Fall.

There are two main poles in Adam Smith's colourful structure of self-interest: human nature and God's providence. In this section we discuss these two poles that support his understanding of self-interest as a way of salvation. We show that self-interest is an innate instinct embedded in human nature by God's providence rather than a human virtue achieved by secular reason as implied in Adam Smith' s thought.

Nature

The good and the bad are intertwined and together form the tapestry of human daily lives. The conflict between these two sides of human nature is well expressed in the confession of Saint Paul, who says 'I know that nothing good lives in me, that is, in my sinful nature. For I have the desire to do what is good, but I cannot carry it out' (Romans 7:18, NIV). The theological question of whether his confession is regarding the human who is yet to be born again is not the main concern here. However, his confession gives us an important clue in exploring Adam Smith's idea of self-interest. Natural instinct based on self-interest is not just an economic issue but also a theological one, because issues such as total depravity and original sin implied in Saint Paul's confession have a theological dimension.

Bernard Mandeville (1670–1733) has proposed that,. even though it could be true that there is nothing good that lives in our sinful nature (as confessed by Saint Paul), it does not necessarily mean, that human depravity needs to be overcome or eliminated in order for salvation to be achieved. The reason is that he believes that our sinful nature leads to public benefits. Note that Mandeville's emphasis on the positive role of self-interest for achieving public benefits is quite different from Adam Smith's in spite of the seemingly similar language. A clear understanding of Mandeville's approach to human nature helps to clarify in two ways Adam Smith's idea of self-interest. First, neither self-denial nor goodness is the way of achieving human virtue and perfection in Mandeville's thought.[5] Second, Mandeville accepts self-interest as a way of human salvation without reservation in spite of his recognition of the vicious side of human nature. He suggests the profound economic insight that self-interest or private vices lead to public benefits.[6]

5 Bernard Mandeville, *Fable of the Bees: Or Private Vices, Publick Benefits. / by Bernard Mandeville with a Commentary Critical, Historical and Explanatory by F.B. Kaye* (Oxford: Clarendon Press, 1924), 323.

6 Ibid., 343–344.

According to Mandeville's argument, the nature of human society is not founded on virtue but on vices. He believes that there is self-love at the centre of all human motives. His ironic and sarcastic argument for self-interest as a way of human salvation gives us an important clue to revealing the multiple colours of self-interest and its role for salvation. In his thought, self-love as the bad and hateful quality of humans is not something to be overcome by virtue; rather, it is the basis of human civilisation. In other words, self-love is not something to be negated or overcome by human reason but to be celebrated as a foundation of salvation for individuals and society.

Therefore, in Mandeville's thought, self-denial or goodness is not the way of achieving human virtue and perfection; rather, self-love as private vice leads to public benefits. This gives rise to the following question: is Mandeville's self-love different from Adam Smith's self-interest? His idea of self-love seems to be reminiscent of Adam Smith's self-interest as both of them argue for the positive role of self-interest for public benefits. However, Adam Smith clearly distances himself from Mandeville.[7] Mandeville's willingness to dissolve the distinctions between vice and virtue is not the only reason why Adam Smith is against this seemingly similar approach to self-interest. There is in fact a fundamental difference between them in terms of their understanding of the nature of human passions. Adam Smith does not believe that human passion is vicious.[8]

Adam Smith uses the language of self-interest in quite a different way from Mandeville. As Waterman (2002) points out, "nature" is one of the most frequently used terms in his *Wealth of Nations*.[9] Self-interest is not a matter of either vice or virtue for Adam Smith, but rather of human nature. Self-interest is the natural desire of bettering one's condition. This approach to self-interest is similar, but subtly different, to that of Mandeville and may offer a clue as to the theological foundations embedded in economic thought.

7 TMS VII.ii.4.6.

8 TMS VII.ii.4.12.

9 A.M.C. Waterman, 'Economics as Theology: Adam Smith's Wealth of Nations', *Southern Economic Journal*, 68/4 (2002), 907–921.

In Adam Smith's system of thought, two main poles support his arguments based on the power of human natural desire. They are human nature and all-ruling providence of God.[10] Whether it be a king or beggar, the human self-conscious desire is a *natural* propensity innate in humans who have an instinct given from the womb. We all have the nature to truck, barter and exchange one thing for another for the individual maximization of self-interest. In Adam Smith's theology of economic life, nature is good as he believes that God's never-failing goodness is imbedded in human nature. Humans are created beings whose behaviour is motivated by self-interest which is an inherent instinct in God's providence, and God is the Creator who is the all-seeing judge of the world with infinite power and wisdom. As shown in these statements and others, it should not be ignored that human nature and God's providence are interrelated, so cannot be separated without damaging the integrity of his systems of thought. The strongest motives for self-interest are prescribed not as virtues or vices but as the natural desire of bettering one's own condition, with this desire coming from womb and never leaving until death. Self-interest is the providence of the infinite goodness of the Creator in his theological system. It seems to be neither possible nor beneficial to separate his concept of self-interest from the broader system of his thought which is believed to be influenced by anthropological and theological paradigms in his own times.

Therefore, in contrast to Mandeville's approach to human nature, Adam Smith's view is that self-interest is not human vice but rather is an expression of God's providence. Thus, this notion of self-interest is built on two theological poles: nature and providence and this raises self-interest to more than economic rationality or moral emotion.

10 TMS VII.iii.3.15; TMS III.5.12.

Two Poles of Adam Smith's Self-interest

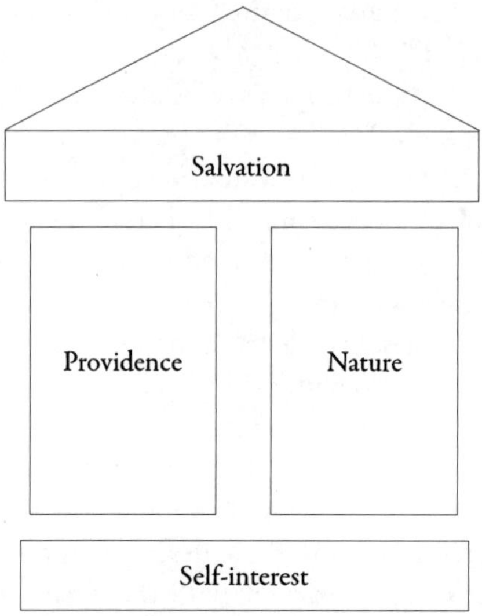

Self-interest is a *natural* instinct *given* by the providential wisdom of God, whose goodness never fails through the invisible hand.

The diagram above shows the structure of self-interest explained in this section. In the centre of Adam Smith's idea of self-interest, we may see that there are two main poles: nature and providence. By assuming that self-interest is a natural desire given in God's providence, Adam Smith adopts a theological approach to an economic behaviour.

Providence

The more important but rarely discussed aspect of self-interest is God's providence. The theological elements and implications are an integral part of human economic behaviour in Adam Smith's thought. Despite his theological approach to self-interest, modern economics has eliminated, perhaps through unconscious neglect, the providential aspect of self-interest. The idea of providence is important not only to understand Adam Smith's thought but also to see the theological dimension of economics more generally.

One of the reasons for the elimination of the theological dimension of human economic behaviour in modern economics may be due to the narrow approach to self-interest as shown in the previous section. In the rational choice theory, for instance, 'rational' means to make choices based upon the goal of maximizing satisfaction. Such economic rationality is calculative and instrumental. Becker is one of the economists who try to extend the rational approach to human behaviour which is traditionally beyond economic analysis.[11] For him, the economic approach is a method of analysis, rather than an assumption about particular motivation. Therefore, the economic analysis is applicable even to value-laden human behaviour including marriage, crime, and politics in Becker's thought. Of course, he does not overlook the various motives of human behaviour beyond self-interest. However, he suggests that the economic approach is not limited to human behaviour based on narrow self-interest.[12] He believes that the economic approach is applicable to all human behaviour in spite of various values and preferences, not because all human behaviour is economic in nature but rather because human behaviour is guided by rational decision-making. In spite of his broad application of the economic approach to human behaviour, a theological dimension of self-interest is missed in his economic approach.

In contrast with the rational approach, Adam Smith believes that the natural instinct of self-interest as human self-conscious desire for happiness is given in God's providence. Self-interest is an instinct that God has provided to facilitate the pursuit of human happiness. Without taking into consideration his theological approach to self-interest, it is not possible to understand properly why Adam Smith suggests this strongest motive of self-interest as a way of salvation for individuals and society. Even though there are no sophisticated theological arguments in his works, there are many clues in his works that reveal how he explains the experiential reality of ordinary people from the perspective of self-interest.

11 Gary Becker, *The Economic Approach to Human Behaviour* (Chicago: University of Chicago Press, 1976), 14.

12 Gary Becker, 'Nobel Lecture: The Economic Way of Looking at Human Behaviour', *Journal of Political Economy*, 101/3 (1993), 385–409.

For Adam Smith, the Creator is always a good God who promotes general order and happiness through his *providence*. This ensures the prosperity and perfection of the great system of *nature*. Even the vices and follies of humankind are a necessary part of God's plan to bring out good from evil in Smith's theological paradigm.[13] These human vices and follies have a role for good in his system of thought, and provide the foundation from which he develops his own theory of human desire of self-interest as a way of salvation. A good God and created humans are likely to have a mutual and common goal of happiness of the whole through the efficient application of self-interest in spite of the seemingly insurmountable gap between the holiness of God and the sinfulness of creatures. The tensional dichotomy of evil and good is not antimony, but it is unified through the providential nature of self-interest in spite of the vices and follies of humankind. Even though the human self-conscious desire of self-interest is a weakness of human beings, it works as a remedy in Adam Smith's theological foundations of economic thought.[14]

Self-interest is not disguised self-love or pride tainted by human sinfulness but is endowed by God's providence for human weakness. Self-interest has no meaning without God's providence, and God's providence has no relation to reality without self-interest in Adam Smith's thought. This inherent drive of self-interest is naturally given rather than rationally acquired. It is a *natural* instinct *endowed* by a benevolent God who works through an invisible hand with providence and design for the harmony and benefit of humankind. Self-preservation is the end which Nature seems to have proposed in the formation of all creatures. Humans are endowed with a very strong desire of those ends, and it has not been entrusted to the slow and uncertain determinations of our reason, to find out the proper means of bringing them about. Nature has directed us to the greater part of these by original and immediate instincts. Adam Smith's idea of self-interest is essentially *natural* in the sense that it is an instinct rather than the slow and uncertain determinations of our reason, and fundamentally *given* in the sense that it is endowed by the Nature rather than acquired by human wisdom.[15]

13 TMS I.ii.3.4.
14 TMS III. 4.6–7.
15 TMS II.i.5.10.

The two main poles that support the uniqueness of his approach to self-interest in his statements quoted above are '*nature*' and '*providence*'. The concept of nature is related to his anthropology of who humans are, while the term providence is related to his theology of the nature of God. The natural desire of bettering one's own condition is the strongest motive of humans, and this comes from God's providence.[16]

In Adam Smith's theology of economics, the human instinct of self-interest is seen as the *nature* of humans endowed by God's *providence*. Therefore, we may conclude that the notion of self-interest as God's providence needs close attention not only in theology and ethics but also in economics. This also gives us insights into the theological dimension of economics in his thought. The providential aspect of self-interest leads us to see that economic ideas are based on theological thought. We may then say that economics is theology.

To sum up, Adam Smith believes that self-interest in bettering one's condition is natural and providential. It is natural as it is embedded in human instinct by Nature, and it is providential in that it is given by the wisdom of God who knows human weakness. Self-interest is not only natural in the sense that it is an innate instinct of humans, but it is also providential as it is given by God whose goodness never fails.

2.2. Self-interest: Human Self-conscious Desire with Various Colours

Adam Smith's self-interest is like a prism through which it is possible to see different colours depending on the angle from which it is viewed. Specifically, there are three different colours, or faces, to Adam Smith's notion of self-interest. In the previous section, it was shown that he viewed self-interest as human nature given by God's providence. In this section it will be shown that self-interest as human nature given by God's providence

16 TMS VII.ii.I.18.

has not only economic and moral characteristics, but also a theological dimension. This triadic approach will help to clarify the meaning and role of self-interest for salvation in Adam Smith's thought.

Economic Dimension of Self-interest

It is generally regarded that Adam Smith believes that self-interest is the primary motivation for individuals in commercial society. Does Adam Smith's self-interest have an economic dimension? If so, is it the same as the economic rationality that has become a cornerstone of modern economics? This is the question which is addressed in this section.

Modern economics, based on a rational approach to human behaviour, puts faith in human rationality as a way of salvation for both individuals and society. Becker is one economist who tries to apply utility maximization to all facets of human behaviour. He makes a distinction between self-interest and utility maximization, taking the view that self-interest is but one of the various human motives conceived by individuals who maximise their welfare. Utility maximization is an economic approach whereas self-interest is seen as one of possibly many motives of human behaviour. This has the effect of broadening the economic approach beyond those traditionally considered by economists to all human behaviour.[17]

Thus, Becker's approach to self-interest is different from Adam Smith's, as the latter believes that self-interest is the innate instinct embedded in human nature by God's providence. Becker agrees that Adam Smith applies the economic approach to human behaviour not only in the market, but also in social and political areas. However, he believes that Adam Smith is not consistent in applying the economic method to all human behaviour as Adam Smith, dismisses certain human behaviour as a result of folly and ignorance. Then the question is: what is 'economic rationality'? What is 'self-interested behaviour'? Does Adam Smith's idea of self-interest have an economic dimension?

17 Gary Becker, *The Economic Approach to Human Behavior* (Chicago: University of Chicago Press, 1976), 12.

We are interested in our own economic happiness, so it is natural to have a strong interest in economic wealth, believing that the richer we are, the happier we will be. It follows that self-interest as a human consciousness certainly has an economic dimension in the sense that humans are economic beings who have an interest in their own economic welfare. Self-interest is indeed the main motive of human economic behaviour in the market.

This economic dimension of self-interest is without doubt the foundation of Adam Smith's approach to human behaviour. People buy and sell goods and services in the commercial market to make a profit. Humans have a natural instinct to be free from poverty by maximising their own wealth. The concept of conscious self-interested behaviour is deeply embedded in modern economic theory. Humans are assumed to have a single-minded pursuit of self-interest and this is represented as a desire to maximise their wealth. The economic approach to self-interest is shown in the axiom of rationality in the neoclassical utility-maximizing framework, which has the human desire of self-interest as a starting point for analyzing economic human behaviour. The economic rationality based on self-interest is one of the essential axioms used to analyze the human behaviour searching for the maximization of their interest in the world of material scarcity. An economic human is assumed to behave rationally to maximize self-interest in the market for secular salvation from poverty in this economic world. Conflict between individual benefit and social welfare, which is caused by a single-minded pursuit of self-interest, is presumed to be harmonized somehow in the free market in which individuals are assumed to have the freedom of fulfilling one's own desire rationally. In the market, the human desire of self-interest is identified with human rationality. Modern economics based on the rational approach to self-interest has faith in human rationality as a way of salvation for both individuals and society.

In the economic approach to self-interest, the self-conscious human desire is regarded as nothing but economic rationality. Self-interest is neither a matter of moral emotion nor a theological faith but a matter of economic rationality. The moral or theological dimension of self-interest is irrelevant, and is replaced with one-dimensional rationality. Society is regarded as a sum of solipsistic individuals who rationally maximise their own self-interest in the market. Altruism is then usually regarded as a concealed or disguised self-interest unless it is irrational.

However, in this narrow approach of defining self-interest to be rational, there is no attempt to first define what is meant by the term "rationality". This approach runs the risk of forcing reality to fit the theory, rather than shaping the theory to fit reality, as this rational self-interest makes sense only in a rational, quantified, static world devoid of many of the real, but messy, aspects of human behaviour. Does economic rationality based on self-interest draw on any aspects of moral emotion and theological faith? How can it explain the behaviour of a holistic human being with body, mind, and spirit? At the centre of those questions there is an important issue regarding the nature of rationality.

Adam Smith's idea of self-interest surely has an economic dimension as it is related to the human economic self-consciousness of bettering one's condition in the market. Thus, self-interest at the centre of economic rationality is a way of salvation for individuals and society.[18] He is then an economist analyzing the motives of human behaviour in the market from the perspective of economic rationality, based on the expression of self-interest. There is no negative connotation in Adam Smith's idea of self-interest; rather, it is an economic self-consciousness in the market. The calculative self-interest as a human self-consciousness is the 'desire of bettering our condition' which 'comes with us from the womb, and never leaves us till we go into the grave'.[19] He is optimistic about the effects of human behaviour motivated by such rational self-interest as he says that economic human behaviour is naturally a bond of union and friendship. Moreover, he argues for individual freedom, saying that humans are left perfectly free to pursue their own interest their own way unless they violate the laws of justice.[20] The main axioms of neo-classical economics such as free choice and utility maximization of individuals in the market are central to his understanding of self-interest. In this vein, his idea of self-interest has an economic dimension as generally believed in modern economics, and furthermore it appears that it is nothing but economic rationality at best or selfishness at worst.

18 WN IV.ii.9.
19 WN II.iii.28.
20 WN IV.ix.51.

However, Adam Smith's self-interest seems to be more than a purely calculative rationality. When he argues for self-interest as an efficient cause for economic salvation, his approach to self-interest is something natural rather than something to be achieved by human will, for he frequently says that self-interest is a natural propensity innate in humans who have an instinct from the womb to truck, barter and exchange one thing for another for the individual maximization of self-interest.[21] Adam Smith's approach to self-interest is close to a natural emotion, in contrast to the practical rationality of modern humanism that is related to modern individualism where individual happiness is given priority over public welfare. Even when he emphasizes human freedom in society, he does not have faith in human wisdom and knowledge.[22] Consequently, it would be reasonable to assume that his idea of self-interest as a natural instinct given by God's providence has an economic dimension of efficiency and desire for wealth, but is not exactly the same as the calculative rationality of modern economics. Adam Smith's self-interest has an economic dimension as economic behaviour in the market and is based on self-interest rather than others-interest. It is, however, more than economic rationality as it seems to be more of a natural instinct than a rational ability.[23] We cannot deny that his idea of self-interest surely has an aspect of the economic rationality described in modern economics, yet more importantly it has a warm and emotional flavour in it. This delicate difference is larger than it may appear. The tension between Adam Smith's natural approach to human desire and modern economics' rational understanding of the human mind is the key element in understanding a variety of ethical criticisms against self-interest without simplifying the various aspects of self-interest.

21 WN I.ii.3.

22 WN IV.ix.51.

23 WN I.ii.2.

Moral Critique of Self-Interest

Human behaviour based on self-interest is, however, frequently criticized as being likely to be associated with moral corruption. This ethical approach to self-interest assumes that altruism or other-interest is different from self-interest, and that other-interest cannot be regarded as concealed or irrational self-interest as generally assumed in mainstream economics. It points out that the real motivation of human behaviour is not just economic but also moral. Wogaman (1986) argues that economic individualism based on self-interest is a half-truth neglecting the social nature of human beings, as self-interest easily gives in to the temptation of attributing their success to their own goodness while seeing character deficiencies at the root of others' failure.[24] Then, the desire of self-interest may be detrimental not only to the common good, but also to individuals. Frey (1996) also points out that the utilitarian morality of our age produces destructive notions of responsibility and personal growth.[25] Alvey (1999) mentions economics as a moral science, saying that a rational dimension of self-interest is necessary but not enough.[26] Those ethical approaches are based on the assumption that self-interest may have economic rationality but is devoid of morality. In those ethical criticisms against economic self-interest there is a division between economic self-interest and moral others-interest.

This moral approach to the role of self-interest for salvation is concerned with the possible conflict between the human self-conscious desire and social welfare. Its main concern is no longer in quantifiable economic utility or interest but in the quality of human life. Modern economics believes that an economic human has the target of maximizing economic utility in the market. In other words, the main concern under this narrow approach to self-interest is economic utility and interest rather than humans

24 Phillip Wogaman, *Economics and Ethics: A Christian Enquiry* (London: SCM, 1986).

25 Donald Frey, 'The Good Samaritan as bad economist: Self-interest in economics and theology', *Cross Currents*, 46/3 (1996), 293–302.

26 James Alvey, 'A Short History of Economics as a Moral Science', *Journal of Markets and Morality*, 2/1 (Spring 1999), 53–73.

as subjects. It may then lead to a wrong impression that happiness is something to be achieved by maximising utility without taking into account the moral and emotional dimension of the subject. This is the point that the ethical approaches make when they criticise the narrow self-interest assumed in modern economics. They believe that salvation or happiness is not just the result of the accumulation of economic wealth, even though the latter may be a necessary and important condition to achieve the former. The main concern of the ethical approaches is not in the object to be achieved but in the subjects who achieve it. It emphasizes that human behaviour cannot be explained sufficiently by economic rationality alone unless its moral dimension is taken into consideration, because profit-seeking easily leads to to a blind selfishness. However, in spite of the importance of this criticism, mainstream economics pays little attention to the moral aspect of self-interest as it views the issue as a matter of moral philosophy rather than of economics. Under the different approaches to self-interest, there is a more fundamental issue of the relationship between rationality and morality. Does economic rationality contain a moral dimension? Is there any relationship between rational mind and moral spirit? Adam Smith's approach to self-interest suggests that self-interest is more than economic rationality. Consequently, we need to pay attention to the moral dimension of self-interest to see the relationship.

Moral Dimension of Self-interest

In the previous section it was shown that Adam Smith's self-interest has an economic dimension, but that it is also more than a calculative rationality as he believes it is a natural instinct and feeling rather than human reason and wisdom. This leads us to see the difference between self-interest as the human self-conscious desire and economic rationality as the main principle of modern economics, and to understand how he introduces self-interest as the strongest motive of human desire for moral relationships. Does self-interest have any moral aspect? If so, how is it related to moral sympathy in the thought of Adam Smith, who is generally hailed as the prophet of the modern economics founded on the single-minded pursuit of individual interest? Certainly, he is a moral philosopher who pays close attention to the moral dimension of human existence as shown in his work *The Theory of Moral Sentiments*. Then how could he harmonize narrow self-interest with moral emotion without neglecting the ethical criticism against a calculative and utilitarian rationality of modern economics? This section argues that Adam Smith's self-interest as an instinct embedded in human nature by God's providence has a moral dimension in the sense that it is a foundation of human relationships. However, Adam Smith also views self-interest as more than human virtue. This is the point to be discussed here in this section.

In his book *The Impartial Spectator*, Raphael (2007) argues that self-interest is not necessarily the foundation of all human action in Adam Smith's thought, and that sympathy is prominent in his ethical theory not as a motive of action but as a constituent of moral judgement. Thus, sympathy is irrelevant to any question of consistency in Smith's views on the motivation of conduct. According to Raphael, economists often mistakenly argue that there is inconsistency between the *Moral Sentiments* and *The Wealth of Nations* about the motivation of human actions.[27] However, the alleged inconsistency between *Moral Sentiments* and *The Wealth of Nations* is entirely a construction of the commentators who try to interpret the two texts from a purely economic perspective without paying proper attention to Adam Smith's ethical theory.

However, in my opinion, the important point is not that the economists' approach is devoid of Smith's ethical theory. In a sense, trying to analyze human behavior from the perspective of self-interest in *Moral Sentiments* is necessary, for Adam Smith views self-interest as a natural instinct given by God's providence which is fundamental to the matter of human relationships. The problem is, however, that self-interest is interpreted as narrow economic rationality not only by the commentators who find an inconsistency in Adam Smith's works, but also by Raphael who argues that sympathy is prominent in his ethics not as a motive of action, but as a constituent of moral judgement, so it is irrelevant to 'any question

27 D.D. Raphael, *The Impartial Spectator: Adam Smith's Moral Philosophy* (Oxford: Clarendon, 2007), 115.

of consistency in Smith's views on the motivation of conduct'.[28] Then, the question is: is Adam Smith's self-interest nothing but an economic rationality different to others-interest such as compassion or benevolence, or does it have a moral dimension?

One example of a systematic explanation of self-interest taking the moral dimension into consideration is from Hirschman (1977). He suggests that Adam Smith builds up a moral system through sympathy, which motivates people to improve their material well-being so that the usual tension between passions is calmed.[29] He appropriately points out that the private interests and passions are not used as antonyms but as synonyms in Adam Smith's works as the pursuit of material interests is not desire condemned as the poisonous sin of greed, but has the role of calming the uncontrollable passions of humans.

However, Hirschman's approach to the tension between self-interest and sympathy in Adam Smith's works seems to neglect the providential nature of self-interest and sympathy. Even though Adam Smith's self-interest has an economic dimension in which the rational, calculative, and calm decision-making occurs, self-interest is an inherent trait given by God's teleological providence. Self-interest is a dynamic feature of humans, motivating ordinary people to develop mutual relationships.

Another systematic approach to self-interest is offered by Myers, who seems to be more keenly aware of the problem arising from the narrow interpretation of Adam Smith in terms of the categories of modern economics.[30] His main argument is that there is a clear connection between the moral principle of sympathy and the desire of trade based on self-interest by showing the evidence of interrelation between the division of labour and his moral philosophy as he quotes Smith's statements regarding the importance of the power of persuasions. Myers' argument for the close relationship between self-interest and sympathy in Adam Smith's thought comes from

28 Ibid., 116.

29 Albert Hirschman, *The Passions and the Interests: Political Arguments for Capitalism before Its Triumph* (Princeton, NJ: Princeton University Press, 1977), 108–111.

30 Milton Myers, *The Soul of Modern Economic Man: Ideas of Self-Interest, Thomas Hobbes to Adam Smith* (Chicago: University of Chicago Press, 1983).

his acute observation of the fact that Adam Smith's works constantly concentrate on human nature. Whether it is sympathy or self-interest, Myers does not lose the point Smith wants to make regarding the nature of the great mob of humankind. Adam Smith is, he argues, a moral philosopher who is a realist as well as an economist, but, most of all, a discoverer of the soul of the modern economic human. He argues that the pivotal role of *nature* in Adam Smith's thought is the clue to finding consistency in the seeming disparity between sympathy and self-interest. His systematic approach to Adam Smith's self-interest pointedly recognizes the importance of nature as the common element in self-interest and sympathy.

Adam Smith, however, believes that moral sentiments originate not from human wisdom but from natural desire as morality is emotion rather than reason. It is self-interest that he has in his mind as the strongest motive of moral sentiments. Such an innate relationship between self-interest and moral sentiments is clearly expressed in his explanation of the natural aspect of self-interested emotion about far-away disasters.[31] The emotional aspect of self-interest is naturally extended to the moral sentiments. He believes that the instinct is not something to be overcome by reason but that is given by nature. In other words, in his explanation of moral behaviour Adam Smith emphasizes that self-interest is the strongest motive of human behaviour in the market, because it is not a blinded self-love but human self-conscious desire without which moral sentiments cannot be brought about.[32] This inner dynamic relationship between self-interest and sympathy leads Adam Smith to be able to make a seemingly conflicting but actually consistent argument in his moral theory.[33] In his approach, we may see his warm attitude toward human weakness. He believes that we are naturally interested in our business rather than others. However, he also believes that such self-interestedness is not an obstacle against human relationships but rather is the essential element of human moral sentiments.[34]

31 TMS III.3.4.
32 TMS III.4.7.
33 TMS VII.ii.3.16.
34 TMS VII.ii.3.15.

Thus, it is reasonable to say that in Adam Smith's thought, self-interest is at the centre of human compassion for others. He believes that self-interest has a moral dimension because moral sentiments are for him nothing but an extension of the human desire of bettering one's condition. According to his theory of moral sentiments, humans are moral beings not in spite of, but because of self-interest. He believes that the human self-conscious desire is the powerful energy that ties individuals together, without which they fall apart. Consequently, for him, morality is nothing but human relationship based on self-interest. There is no moral sympathy without self-interest as self-interest is a binding force that connects individuals.

Then the question to be asked is: how can Adam Smith's moral dimension of self-interest answer those ethical criticisms such as the neglect of the social nature of human beings and the destructive utilitarian morality? There are three points to be mentioned in explaining how he harmonizes narrow self-interest with moral emotion. Adam Smith believes that self-interest is neither a selfishness that is a blind self-love, nor a self-negligence that is to be blamed, nor a virtue that is to be achieved by human wisdom, but rather is an imaginary change of situations with others.

Firstly, Adam Smith's self-interest has a moral dimension. It is not a disguised selfishness as assumed by ethical criticisms but an imaginary change of situations with others. Desire for bettering one's condition by exchange is introduced again in his moral sentiments.[35] Sympathy as imaginary exchange in the imaginary market of his moral system is the exact counterpart of trade and barter in the practical market in his economic system. His idea of self-interest is the strongest motive not only in the economic market of commodities but also in an imaginary exchange of sentiments. Thus, in his thought, self-interest has a moral dimension as it is at the centre of moral sentiments. It does not neglect the social nature of human beings as it is an imaginary change of situations with others.

Secondly, Adam Smith's self-interest has a moral dimension, yet it is not a rational virtue to be achieved by human wisdom but rather an immediate

35 TMS VII.iii.I.4.

sense and feeling which all humans are given by nature.[36] Adam Smith's moral dimension of self-interest is then not a matter of virtues or vices, for he believes that the moral emotion based on self-interest is not confined to virtuous humans but given as a principle in human nature even to the most hardened violator of the laws of society.[37] Adam Smith's self-interest has a moral dimension in it, but he does not approach it from a dichotomy of virtues or vices. Self-interest as a motive of moral sentiments is a synthetic effort to overcome the tension between virtues and vices in an experiential reality of the daily lives of common people. Adam Smith's idea of self-interest has a moral dimension not because his sympathy is grounded in self-interest as a virtue to be realized by human wisdom, but because it is an essential part of human nature. Thus, it is reasonable to say that Adam Smith's self-interest has a moral dimension as it is the strongest motive of moral sentiments. It is not the destructive utilitarian morality based on economic rationality but an imaginary change of situations with others.

Thirdly, Adam Smith's self-interest has a moral dimension, for it is not just the matter of having interests, but also the matter of preserving the self as subject.[38] His moral approach to self-interest turns our concerns from *interests* to the *self*. According to a story in the Bible, a rich man who stores up possessions for himself but is not rich towards God is described as a fool who does not know that the meaning of life is not in the abundance of his possessions (Luke 12:16–21 NIV). The biblical theme is clearly shown in Adam Smith's sympathy as he says that not vanity or trinkets but ease and tranquillity are the great and ultimate objects of all humans who have a self-conscious desire for salvation.[39] Adam Smith surely understands that salvation is not a matter of material interests but rather a matter of the self. If salvation is self-preservation in this world or in a world to come, his moral dimension of self-interest is the natural and efficient cause for the final happiness as it takes into account the importance of the self without

36 TMS VII.iii.2.8.
37 TMS I.i.I.1.
38 TMS II.i.5.10.
39 TMS IV.i.8.

neglecting material interests. There is no division between the self and interests in his moral approach to self-interest. Therefore, we may say that Adam Smith's self-interest as natural instinct given by God's providence is the strongest motive of human desire not only in the market but also in moral relationships. This does not neglect the social nature of human beings or fall into the destructive utilitarian morality as self-interest here is an imaginary change of situations with others.

Theological Dimension of Self-interest

It is true that we all have a natural interest in the eternality of our life, and it is also true that self-interest is generally accepted as an obstacle against salvation in religious and theological circles. Does self-interest have a theological dimension in Adam Smith's thought? This is the question discussed here in this section. It will be argued that Adam Smith's self-interest as an instinct embedded in human nature by God's providence has a theological dimension as it is the theological foundation of a human relationship with God in Adam Smith's thought. Self-interest is the providential gift for human weakness by the all-powerful God whose goodness never fails in the world and in a world to come.

In spite of its importance in understanding the meaning of religious salvation, the theological dimension of self-interest is one of the most neglected ideas in modern economics and theology. Viner pointedly says that modern economics does not pay attention to the religious and theological aspect of its foundation.[40] However, we also need to emphasize the fact that the economic elements and implications which should be an integral part of religious behaviour are not given proper attention in modern theology. There is a bifurcation between economics and theology. What is the main cause of the division between the two? Why are the religious elements and implications erased from modern economics? Why is Christian

40 Jacob Viner, *The Role of Providence in the Social Order* (Philadelphia, PA: American Philosophical Society, 1972), 81.

theology not concerned about a possible role of self-interest as a way of salvation? Is it because the theological dimension of self-interest is missed in both economics and theology? This is the main concern of this section, although a detailed discussion will be saved for the following chapters. This section will simply show that Adam Smith's self-interest has a theological dimension, which serves as preparation for further discussion.

One of the reasons why the theological aspect of self-interest is missed or neglected in economics and theology could be the tension between economic rationality and religious faith. Knight's argument is a good example showing how one may approach the moral aspect of self-interest without taking into consideration the theological dimension.[41] Without the theological dimension of self-interest, it is inevitable for him to conclude that the teachings of Christianity provide little or no guidance for change and improvement in social organization as he presumes that the social reform is the result of a positive effort to keep emotions and religion out of debate. In spite of his keen concern about the moral dimension of rationality, he seems to neglect the theological dimension of the self-conscious desire on which modern economics is believed to stand.

In contrast, however, the dichotomy between economic rationality and religious faith is overcome in Adam Smith, who believes that the moral aspect of self-conscious desire has a theological dimension. He says that 'we necessarily pursue the most effectual means for promoting the happiness of mankind, and may therefore be said, in some sense, to co-operate with the Deity, and to advance as far as in our power the plan of Providence…'[42] His self-interest as the strongest motive of moral relationships with others is extended again to a theological level.

Adam Smith's self-interest is like a rainbow showing different colours depending on which perspective we take. One of the colours innate to his self-interest is related to his religious faith. Adam Smith's self-interest has a theological dimension because it is his religious faith in the goodness of God. His idea of self-interest is a religious self-consciousness as he believes

41 Frank H. Knight, 'Ethics and Economic Reform: Christianity', *Economica*, 6 (November 1939), 398–422.

42 TMS III.5.7.

that it is given by God's providential grace. If we look at his self-interest from a theological perspective, his conception of self-interest has a clear and consistent colour of religious faith.

His approach to human behaviour from the focal point of self-interest has different colours and shapes from just calculative rationality or emotional sympathy. The human self-conscious desire of self-interest has a theological origin coming from Adam Smith's religious belief in humans as created beings, the world with an eschatological hope, and God with providence. In that sense, he is a theologian analyzing the structure of faith in human behaviour using the idea of self-interest. Adam Smith believes that humans are created in the image of God, and have the desire of bettering our condition that comes with us from the womb.[43]

In addition, more importantly, such a hope or expectation is deeply rooted in human nature as shown in Adam Smith's statement that 'Our happiness in this life is thus, upon many occasions, dependent upon the humble hope and expectation of a life to come: a hope and expectation deeply rooted in human nature; which can alone support its lofty ideas of its own dignity….'[44] However, this unsatisfying desire for happiness in this life is, according to him, ultimately dependent on eschatological faith in a life to come, when exact justice will be done to every human. He argues that 'an All-powerful Being, who watches over our conduct, and who, in a life to come, will reward the observance, and punish the breach of them…'[45] These statements may show that he has a clear vision of eschatological and teleological hope in the future without losing sight of the reality of God's providence over the world.

In these theologically orientated arguments, we can conclude that self-interest again is at the centre of Adam Smith's theological approach to human behaviour, as more clearly shown in his saying that the propriety of reverence to the infinite goodness of his Creator is well supported by the strongest motives of self-interest. Virtue is weak, and passions are unstable; however, humans are created to have stronger and more stable instincts

43 TMS III.2.31.

44 TMS III.ii.33.

45 TMS III.5.12.

given by the benevolent God, that is, for Smith, self-interest. The theological dimension of self-interest unifies the tension between virtues and vices. Even in his theological approach to human behaviour, the central role of self-interest is not eliminated; rather, it is emphasized as God's providence in his system. Therefore, he is a theologian who knows the weakness of common people as *creatures*, but does not turn a blind eye to the infinite goodness of God, the *Creator*. In his system of thought, moral sympathy and practical self-interest stand on the same horizon of religious faith through the strongest human motive of the desires of self-interest, which is inherent in human *nature* by God's *providence*. It should be emphasized that this works as a whole, not separately, in his all arguments.

To sum up, Adam Smith's self-interest has in essence a theological flavour as he believes that self-interest is a natural instinct embedded in human nature by God's providence. Whether he is an orthodox Christian or deist is not the main issue here in this section as it mainly depends on which theology we adopt. The point is that his self-interest has a theological origin, and its theological dimension is the foundation of his economic ideas. Adam Smith's self-interest is neither purely mathematical calculation, nor morally distorted selfishness, nor religiously condemned self-love. Rather, it is practical rationality, emotional sympathy, and religious faith in his system of thought. They are inter-connected to each other and thus cannot be divided separately without distorting his argument. The originality of his analysis of self-interest lies in his synthesis. He describes an ordinary and real motive of human behaviour of common people, taking into consideration an economic, moral and theological side of human existence in the daily lives of the great mob of humans. He does not neglect the tensions between value and fact, virtue and vices, rationality and emotions, body and soul, reason and faith, heaven and earth, grace and nature, theory and fact, salvation and sin, transcendent and immanent, eternal and transient, this life and a life to come etc. In his approach to self-interest, calculative reason, emotional sympathy, and religious faith are intertwined. We can see different faces of the human instinct of self-preservation embedded in his self-interest. The traditional tension between virtues and vices of humans is overcome and turns into a dynamic motive of human behaviour in his system of thought founded on self-interest.

2.3. Self-interest as a Way of Salvation

In the previous sections, it is shown that Adam Smith's notion of self-interest is founded on two important poles of nature and providence. From this foundation, it is argued that self-interest is more than economic rationality, moral depravity, or the consequence of the Fall as it has economic, moral, theological dimensions in his thought. However, the neglect of the social nature of human beings is not the only criticism against the possible weakness of self-interest. MacIntyre (1981) and Milbank (1990) are the focus of this section as their critiques of the role of self-interest are more fundamental and theological. In this section, it will be shown that Adam Smith's self-interest is a way of salvation.

Self-interest and Telos

MacIntyre argues that an autonomous human has no future because there is no telos in the human autonomy based on self-interest.[46] According to his critique, human self-autonomy rejects any teleological view of humans. His critique comes from a philosophical perspective where rational self-interest has neither virtue nor future because it has no essence that defines the true purpose of humans. He argues that we need the divine law requiring a new kind of respect and awe rather than the self-autonomy based on self-interest. He believes that the true end of humans can no longer be completely achieved in this world. According to his philosophical critique against the rationality of self-interest, Adam Smith is then regarded as a deist rather than a Christian as Adam Smith's moral philosophy is based on self-command which enables us to control our passions when virtue is required for the pursuit of social welfare.[47] His conclusion is that self-interest fails because it has no teleological virtue that leads to the future.

46 Alasdair Macintyre, *After Virtue – a Study in Moral Theory* (London: Duckworth, 1981), 52.

47 Ibid., 218.

Similarly, Long (2000) also says that the modern rationality dissolves all goodness and beauty into material interests so it lacks the virtue of having faith in God, the ultimate end.[48] The point of these critiques is not just the negative side of self-interest but the essential blindness of the human rationality based on self-interest. According to these critiques, virtue and autonomous reason are two different faces of self-interest. If we follow the human self-autonomy of self-interest, according to these critiques there is no salvation for individuals and society because there is no future and telos in rational self-interest.

These arguments against human self-conscious desire are different from the approach that criticizes the moral depravity of selfishness, because its main concern is not in fixing the negative side of self-interest, but in questioning the essence of the human self-conscious desire of rational self-interest itself. This critique brings up the question of the validity of human autonomy, arguing that it has no future because there is no virtue and telos in autonomous reason. According to the critique, self-interest is merely a blind expression of reason of autonomous humans. This approach is not just against the faulty side of self-interest, but it denies self-interest itself. There is no possibility of self-interest being a way of salvation. The core of this critique is then the question of whether self-interest has virtue or a teleological future. Does self-interest have future and telos, or is it blind rationality of human self-autonomy?

Self-interest, for Adam Smith, is natural instinct coming from the womb; however, he is keenly aware of the weakness of human nature, and does not put faith in either uncertain determination of our reason or delusions of self-love. Moreover, he believes that Nature has lit up a stronger power in the human heart that is capable of counteracting the strongest impulses of self-love. Adam Smith has faith in the providential guidance of human nature, saying that 'every part of nature, when attentively surveyed, equally demonstrates the providential care of its Author, and we may admire the wisdom and goodness of God even in the weakness and folly of man.'[49]

48 Stephen Long, *Divine Economy: Theology and the Market* (London: Routledge, 2000), 240.

49 TMS II.iii.3.2.

Self-interest, in Adam Smith's thought, is therefore not sufficiency of self-autonomy but weakness of human nature in God's providence. He sees self-interest as a way for achieving individual happiness and public welfare, not because of its sufficiency of self-autonomy but because of its weakness in need of God's providence. Consequently, Adam Smith's self-interest is different from MacIntyre's moral virtue, because the latter's virtue is something to be *acquired* and *possessed* in order to transform human nature as it happens to be into human nature that could realize its telos. However, the self-interest inherent in human nature possesses telos since it is *naturally endowed* by God's *providence* in Adam Smith's moral system. In this sense, Adam Smith's self-interest has the telos of MacIntyre as it originates from outside of human nature, given by God's providence, but it is different from MacIntyre's telos as Adam Smith's telos is not something to be acquired or possessed but rather is something natural to be endowed by God's providence. MacIntyre seems to neglect the relation between nature and providence in considering Adam Smith's notion of self-interest. Adam Smith's self-interest has its own telos in God's providence.

Self-interest and Gift

A more theologically orientated view based on the theological beauty of God's grace comes from Milbank. He argues that MacIntyre's moral virtue is not sufficient in refuting secular reason, for human autonomy is only a myth which cannot be refuted but out-narrated by a better story. He believes that circulation of the conflict of virtue cannot be overcome by virtue.[50] For him, virtue is a gracious free gift rather than a possession or reward to be acquired from competition for scarce resources. Adam Smith's self-interest and MacIntyre's telos-based virtue are again challenged by Milbank in terms of the lack of grace. This critique is different from the previous criticisms suggested from moral and philosophical perspectives because its main concern is neither in fixing the faulty side of self-interest,

50 John Milbank, *Theology and Social Theory: Beyond Secular Reason* (Oxford: Basil Blackwell, 1990).

nor in pointing out the blindness of human autonomy based self-interest. It comes rather from a theological perspective that salvation is neither the matter of selfish achievement nor human virtue, but a gift from God who gives freely.

In his *Theology and Social Theory*[51] Milbank argues that MacIntyre's moral virtue is insufficient to refute secular reason, because he believes that human autonomy is a myth which cannot be refuted but only be out-narrated by a better story. Virtue is, according to Milbank's theological critique, another conflict as long as it is a matter of overcoming less virtue. The circulation of conflict of virtue cannot be overcome by virtue, so he argues that virtue is not such a scarce resource as assumed in the modern naked competition in capitalism. Therefore, according to Milbank, MacIntyre's argument of virtue as a reward for excellence rather than a free gift is neither socialist nor Christian. By arguing for a theological dimension of self-interest, he completely disconnects the self from interest, connected connection which is clear in MacIntyre's argument of rewarding virtue. According to Milbank, virtue is not the self-interest of human beings but a gift from God, so there is no possibility of self-interest being a competitive virtue at all. Following this line of argument, he concludes that capitalism based on rational self-interest is a heresy celebrating human autonomy, which is motivated by will for interest, and not by a true, good, and beautiful gift from God because human economic behaviour is not aesthetic or liturgical work offered to God but a sacrifice made by one's will for wages as a reward. This critique stands on a different horizon from the economical and philosophical approaches mentioned in the previous sections. According to Milbank's theological critique, human autonomy based on rational self-interest has neither virtue nor future; therefore, it is heretical.

The issue of this theological critique against self-interest is then the question of whether self-interest is a gift from God. Is self-interest a gift to be given freely, or is it rather heretical and secular? This is the question

51 The second edition of his book *Theology and Social Theory: Beyond Secular Reason* was published in 2006. The page number is from the first edition as its content is almost the same as the second edition except the introduction.

coming from the theological critique against self-interest. It is an important question as it points out the weakness of secular reason itself from a theological perspective. The relationship between self-interest and salvation cannot be properly illuminated without answering the question. It is also a difficult question to answer as it is basically a matter of theological faith and hence beyond purely rational discussion. However, the clarification of the theological structure of self-interest hidden in Adam Smith's thought may help in searching for an answer.

MacIntyre argues that virtue should come from outside of individual autonomy and be teleological, while Milbank believes that such a telos-based virtue even coming from outside is still problematic because such a moral precept is in danger of being devoid of the grace of God. For Milbank, a true virtue is a gift which is neither an economic rationality to be acquired inside of the self, nor a moral virtue to be acquired from outside of the self; rather, it is to be given as a free gift rather than as trade. Then the question is whether self-interest has a dimension of gift or grace in Adam Smith's moral system. Adam Smith's self-interest is not something to be acquired either from inside or outside, but it is a natural gift endowed by the benevolent Creator.[52]

Contrary to Milbank's criticism against self-interest or virtue, Adam Smith believes that the human self-conscious desire of self-interest does not dissolve goodness and beauty into a distorted self-love; rather, self-interest originates from the goodness of God as Nature has directed us by original and immediate instinct. Of course, gifts are likely to be another kind of economic trade working as inducements based on self-interest in Adam Smith's free market because we may give gifts in expectation of receiving something in return. However, we are able to expect them in pleasure and joy with hope and faith in the world to come. MacIntyre seems to overlook the relation between human nature and God's providence in Smith's self-interest. Self-interest may be a grace and gift in God's providence in Smith's theology. Adam Smith's self-interest is *natural* rather than *rational*. Self-interest, for Smith, is innately already in human nature as the strongest motive.

52 TMS II.i.5.10.

For MacIntyre, the axiom of individual autonomy has no future or telos unless its rationality has an ethical precept coming from outside of self-sufficiency. On the contrary, for Milbank, virtue cannot be grace no matter where it comes from. In his theological paradigm, salvation is not to be *acquired* by virtue no matter how high it is. For him, truth is theological beauty and grace. It is not human reason but God's grace that is the only way to salvation for individuals and society, so Milbank rejects Macintyre's argument as not Christian. God's grace is the world of affluence, not of scarcity, so he can continue to say that God's relationship with humans is based on gift rather than trade, rejecting economic rationality as heretical because it presumes a utility-maximising autonomous individual whose relationship is not based on gifts but on trade.

However, Adam Smith's approach may not be dispatched either by MacIntyre's argument that moral virtue comes from outside of self-sufficiency or Milbank's theological argument that grace is a gift. Adam Smith begins from his faith that self-interest is inherent human *nature* endowed by God's *providence*. Self-interest is naturally inherent in human instinct; however, it is not self-sufficient but comes from outside of self-autonomy. Self-interest is endowed from outside; however, it is not by trade but as a gift from God's providence. Virtue and rationality are to be acquired and achieved by human wisdom rather than given naturally, while human wisdom is, for Adam Smith, God's wisdom in its essence. Adam Smith believes that human wisdom, if any, comes from God. Self-interest is not a result of human wisdom but a gift from God's wisdom, not something to be acquired by human reason, but endowed by God's providence.

Various critiques of self-interest come from different perspectives. Each critique is based on its own paradigm, so each may have a limited validity in analyzing self-interest. Adam Smith's approach to self-interest includes three main entities, which are individuals as subjects, community as the world, and God as the Creator. If Knight criticises the lack of reality in Christian love, then Adam Smith may say that the self-interest on which modern economics is believed to stand on is essentially a moral relationship with others coming from self-love. Wogaman's ethical critique against the weakness of human self-centeredness that easily falls into blind selfishness[53] is not neglected in Adam Smith's idea of self-interest, which has three levels of moral structure as discussed by Halteman.[54] If self-interest is criticized for its weakness of falling into selfishness, Adam Smith may come forward with the bond and union of friendship of trade and a moral system of sympathy, the impartial spectator, and the still-higher tribunal.[55] Solipsistic selfishness may be corrected into relational union through self-interest in the market through which Adam Smith believes that even the smallest parts are fitted to one another and will contribute to compose one immense and connected system.[56] If Milbank points out the limitation of human virtue as a way of salvation and suggests a theological interpretation of trade in terms of a gracious free gift rather than the narrow selfishness of contract, then Adam Smith observes the instability and ineffectiveness of both human passion and virtue. He may speak about the inherent instinct of self-interest given by divine providence, which may be, for him, a higher dimension of inherent human quality than the 'feeble effort of human reason' and the 'uncertain determination of our reason'.[57] A divinely given instinct of self-interest may guide the tension between passion and virtue into harmony. If self-interest is criticised as heretical secular reason from a Christian point of view, as argued by MacIntyre who talks about the lack of teleology in human autonomous reason from an eschatological perspective of salvation, note that Adam Smith does not put faith in feeble human reason; he may instead say that self-interest is a providential gift as embedded in human instinct and that God guides this self-interest by the invisible hand making 'ample provision for remedying many of the bad effects of the folly and injustice of man'.[58]

53 J. Phillip Wogaman, *Economics and Ethics: A Christian Enquiry* (London: SCM Press, 1986).

54 James Halteman, 'Is Adam Smith's Moral Philosophy an Adequate Foundation for a Market Economy?' *Markets and Morality*, 6/2 (2003), 453–478.

55 TMS IV.iii.c.9; TMS III.2.33–34; TMS III. 3.20–23, 28–29.

56 WN II.ii.13–16.

57 WN V.i.g.24–25; TMS II.i.5.8–10.

58 WN IV.ix.28.

In short, in Adam Smith's theology of economic life, the desire of the single minded pursuit of self-interest is human nature given by God's providence. The desire of self-interest is neither a moral failure nor religious disobedience. Humans are born with the natural self-consciousness of bettering one's condition for their own happiness. In his theology of economics, the seemingly economic behaviour is in essence related to a theological faith. It would be inaccurate to describe Adam Smith's self-interest as purely a matter of human autonomy without a theological dimension. He believes that 'all the events in this world were conducted by the providence of a wise, powerful, and good God, and we might be assured that whatever happened tended to the prosperity and perfection of the whole'.[59] Adam Smith's faith that self-interest is inherent in human nature by God's providence is pivotal to his whole system of thought, including all human behaviour, whether it be economic, moral or religious. Human self-interest without God's providence has no meaning at all. Self-interest is therefore a way of salvation in Adam Smith's thought.

2.4. Adam Smith's Theology of Economics

In the previous section, it is shown that self-interest is a way of salvation in Adam Smith's thought as it is a natural instinct given as the providential gift by the grace of God whose goodness never fails. Adam Smith is a theologian, who puts the human desire of self-interest at the centre of God's providence in the world. His political economics is in essence a theological investigation of the economic world of his own time. However, the theological foundations of his economic thoughts are not explicit in his works. Imagination is sometimes very useful in understanding the reality of men, the world, and God as it may help us become free from the boundaries of reality. If humans are the image of the invisible God, then we may need

59 TMS VII.ii.I.18.

theological imagination to see the reality of the invisible God. Likewise, we need imagination to approach the theology that is implicit in Adam Smith's works, for he observes human behaviour through the colourful prism of self-interest without depending on theological terms.

In *The Wealth of Nations*, Adam Smith analyzes the economic dimension of human self-consciousness in the market. Like many other modern economists, he is also concerned about the conflict and harmony between individual self-interest and social welfare. How to harmonize the powerful but selfish self-interest and the abstract but essential social welfare is one of the main issues he addresses in his analysis of economic behaviour in the market. However, in his economic thought, the human desire for pursuing one's own self-interest, expressed as economic self-consciousness in the market, is not only economic behaviour but also has a moral dimension of sympathy. In his moral approach to the economic self-consciousness of humans, there are theological foundations. If we approach Adam Smith's economic thoughts without taking his theological precepts into account, we inevitably truncate his thoughts into our own world-view, which may be heavily influenced by the one-dimensional perception of rationality in our own time.

There are three main theological precepts we need to recognize in his theological foundations of economic thought: God, the world, and human beings. First, God is assumed to be all-powerful, all-knowing, always good, transcendent over the world and interested in the economy of the world. If salvation is a matter of being with God, it is natural for Adam Smith to believe that our salvation is not in this world but in a world to come. Second, this world is the place where God's invisible providence and good grace rules over the vices and follies of humankind. If this world is the place of vanity, it is natural for Adam Smith to argue that this world is transitory rather than eternal. Third, humans are born with the instinctive desire of bettering one's own condition, which is God's gift. If the natural instinct of humans is related to the grace of God, then it is natural for him to believe that the desire of self-interest is at the centre of human freedom and will. Adam Smith's economic thought is related to these theological foundations. Natural self-interest is a window through which we can see his theological foundations of economic thought.

God, Humans, and the World

God is the most important theological background we can see through the prism of Adam Smith's self-interest. One of the main theological foundations of his economic thought is his idea of the transcendent God. In his theology, God is 'an All-powerful Being, who watches over our conduct, and who, in a life to come, will reward the observance, and punish the breach of them'.[60] He believes that God is the Creator, and human beings are created in God's own image. This religious faith is the main theme that permeates all his thoughts. We need theological imagination as there is no systematic approach to God in his works except some traditional images such as all-knowing, all-powerful, and never-failing goodness.[61] In Adam Smith's image of God, God is not only a transcendent being but also a person who has an interest in the happiness of human beings, just as humans beings have an interest in their own happiness in this world and in a world to come. God is concerned about the economy of the world, but he presides over the world by the invisible hand since God is transcendent. Therefore, according to Adam Smith's theological beliefs, this world is transient, and the true happiness of human beings is only possible in a life to come when we are with God. He argues that humans are limited and imperfect beings, so they are required to obey God who is infinite, incomprehensible and perfect. Men as created beings are absolutely dependent on God the Creator whose goodness never fails. This relationship between God and humans beings is the centre of Adam Smith's theological foundations.

The insurmountable gap between God's holiness and human weakness is a typical theme shown in mainstream Christian theologies, especially in the dialectical theology of neo-orthodoxy associated with Barth and Brunner. Adam Smith as a theologian, however, tries to bridge this gap by connecting God's providence and human nature through the natural self-conscious desire of humans. Self-interest, in his theology, is inherent human nature endowed by God's providence. The difference between God and men is constantly not only emphasized, but also harmonized in his argument that God is all-powerful, all-knowing, and always good.

60 TMS.III.5.12.

61 TMS VII.ii.3.20.

One of the many aspects we can see through the prism of Adam Smith's self-interest is that human self-conscious desire is the gift of God whose goodness never fails. Adam Smith's God is transcendent over the world and human beings are here in this world. If so, are human beings then left alone? Adam Smith believes that God's goodness never leaves us alone. One of God's gifts given to humans is the self-conscious desire of self-interest. It is a gift as it is free and good. Adam Smith argues that the pursuit of self-interest has nothing to do with a blind selfishness because the natural desire of human self-interest is given by God whose goodness never fails. Theological imagination is required at this stage to see the colour of his theology coming through the prism of his religious faith in God's providence and human nature. He agrees with the contemporary theologians that humans are created in the image of God. However, he seems to concentrate on the weakness of humans rather than the power of reason when interpreting the theological meaning of the image of God. Humans are aware of the littleness of their being. However, weakness of humans may not be God's punishment; rather, it is a place to experience the benevolence of God. Human weakness is not disconnection from God; rather, it is used as the bridge by which God is able to come into the daily matters of ordinary people, and they may have faith in God's teleological future with an eschatological hope in the world to come.[62] This grand plan of God's providential design through human weakness seems to be related to his own interpretation of the meaning of the image of God.

At the centre of his theological arguments, there is his faith in the role of self-interest as a way of salvation. Self-interest is not a blind selfishness of human weakness, rather it is the providential nature endowed by God's benevolence for fellowship and union with God to overcome the infinite difference between God and his creatures. Self-interest is not something to be achieved by human wisdom, but a gift from God.

Consequently, Smith's God is transcendent rather than immanent in the sense that in his theological world God is all-knowing, all-powerful and always good, presiding over the created world. Of course, we could say that God's immanence is not completely ignored in his theology of economics. He has a theological idea of the invisible hand, which might be assumed to

62 TMS III.ii.33.

be an immanent aspect of God's intervention in human history. However, Smith's God is transcendent, rather than an immanent being as he believes that this world is transitory. This transient world cannot be the place where the eternal God rests. Humans are, however, not left alone in spite of God's transcendence. Self-interest is the connecting point between humans on earth and God in heaven.

Human Weakness as God's Grace

Through the window of self-interest, we can see another theological foundation of Adam Smith's economic thought. That is, God's grace embedded in human weakness. He believes that self-interest is the grace of God who knows human weakness. The wisdom of humans is in reality God's wisdom. The human self-conscious desire of self-interest is not the power of human wisdom but the weakness of human nature. However, God's grace is sufficient for us, for God's goodness is shown in our weakness. Therefore Adam Smith could say that self-interest as the weakness of human nature is the power of God's wisdom.

Human weakness as God's grace is one of the main themes frequently mentioned in the Bible as shown in the confession that 'I boast all the more gladly about my weaknesses, so that Christ's power may rest on me. That is why, for Christ's sake, I delight in weaknesses, in insults, in hardships, in persecutions, in difficulties. For when I am weak, then I am strong' (2 Corinthians 12:9–10). The human natural esteem of trinkets, vanity, and wealth at the cost of hard work may be a proof of human weakness from a moral standpoint; however, as Adam Smith believes, the seeming moral weakness is paradoxically a proof of the providence of God in a theological dimension as shown even in the weakness of the church and clergy's vanity in his time.[63] Adam Smith's self-interest is reminiscent of the biblical theme that God's power is made perfect in human weakness. Self-interest as a common experience of ordinary people is not just a matter of moral sympathy or economic rationality in Adam Smith' theology, but also reflects God's grace in human weakness, for he believes that the strongest motive

63 WN V.i.g.25.

of self-interest given by the infinite goodness of the Creator never leaves us until we die. Then it is natural for him to say that this unsatisfied desire for happiness in this life is dependent on the humble hope and expectation of a life to come.[64] Self-interest is not any more a matter of virtue or vice, rationality or irrationality; rather, it is human weakness dependent on God. Human weakness is God's grace.

His consistent emphasis on the role of self-interest as a way of individual satisfaction and public wealth comes from his faith in God's grace in human weakness. Adam Smith knows the weakness of the great mob of people, so he constantly comes back to their weakness and God's goodness to find the teleological role of their weakness as a way of salvation in the broader picture of God's providence. Then the mistake of eliminating the religious element of faith in God from his thought leaves nothing but just the irony of human weakness in his works. It is a human weakness assumed in self-interest to be able to see only a part, not the whole. The littleness of humans is one of the main themes flowing through his entire works. However, this human weakness is not a curse but a blessing. Human weakness of self-interest is God's grace.

Self-interest as Relational Rather Than Solipsistic

Adam Smith's self-interest is not solipsistic but relational. The concept of relationships is one of the pivotal attributes of the colourful faces of his self-interest that has three dimensions of rationality, sympathy, and faith. Self-interest as a calculative rationality is the economic relationship of the self with interests. Certainly there is no doubt that Smith's self-interest is individual; however, it is not solipsistic but relational. Even in human selfishness, he believes that 'there are evidently some principles in his nature, which interest him in the fortune of others, and render their happiness necessary to him, though he derives nothing from it except the pleasure of seeing it'.[65]

64 WN IV.ii.9, TMS III.ii.33, TMS IV.i.10.

65 TMS I.i.I.1.

For Adam Smith, social welfare is not just a utilitarian sum of solipsistic self-interests, but a mutual interrelationship among relational individuals. Of course, there is an individual character of human existence in his self-interest as he argues that we do not expect our dinner from the benevolence of others but from their regard towards their own self-interest. However, commerce, for Smith, is not selfishness but a bond of union and friendship. Self-interest is fundamentally relational among the self, others, and God in his works. The market is a place of union and friendship among mutually interdependent individuals. Humans are essentially social beings in mutual relationships.

Self-interest as emotional sympathy is the moral relationship of self with others. He believes that a human relationship with others has emotional sentiments in sympathy that is a natural principle rendering others' happiness into my own self-interest and preparing oneself for others' happiness. This economic and emotional relationship with others in sympathy gets stronger by an inner relationship between the human without and the human within, which is a moral mechanism in oneself, motivated by self-interest, guiding the exterior and rational relationship among ordinary men so that a delusion of self-love does not harm the relationship with others in sympathy.

Self-interest as a religious faith is the theological relationship of the self with God. Adam Smith's self-interest has teleological faith in the religious relationship between men and God; the economic and moral relationship with others finds its final end in our faithful and hopeful relationship with God as he believes that our happiness in this life is dependent on the humble hope and expectation of a life to come. This hope is deeply rooted in human nature in the relationship with the goodness of God. However, it must be emphasised that there is self-interest at the centre of all relationships among self, others, and God in Adam Smith's works.

The providential relationship between God and humans through the natural self-interest endowed by God is the peak of the relational aspect of self-interest. Self-negligence is, therefore, not just morally wrong; it has a religious dimension of disobedience because self-interest is a providential gift naturally given to humans by God's wisdom. If sin is disobedience against God, then self-negligence might be sin in Adam Smith's system.

From the relationship with God, other relationships such as the economic relationship with others and the moral relationship with the human within become an effective way to happiness in God's providence that humans are strong in their weakness, and that humans are weak in their strength. In awareness of the real littleness of ourselves, we find the benevolence of God. The relationship with God embedded in the providential nature of self-interest leads other relationships into the teleological future planned by God who holds the key to prosperity and perfection of the whole. Without the relationship with God, self-interest is not an effective cause but is rather a folly of humankind devoid of telos. By God's providence, self-interest becomes the natural centre of balance or gravity of the triangular relationship among self, others and God with sympathy, reason, and faith as three vertices because self-interest is not the final end to be achieved by human wisdom or reason, but the efficient cause to be endowed by God's wisdom or providence for the final cause of happiness of the whole. Self-interest is providential nature for both human dependence on goodness of God and intervention of God in the world; therefore, it is the contact point between the weakness of creatures and the infinite Creator in his thought. Individuals are not solipsistic but relational with the Creator through self-interest.

Religious Institutions and Self-interest

Another theological issue we can see through the prism of Adam Smith's self-interest is religion. In religion it seems to be generally assumed that self-sacrifice and self-negation are more emphasized as a way of salvation than is the pursuit of self-interest and self-love. It may be true in this self-oriented society that we cannot love God and our neighbours unless we deny ourselves. However, in Adam Smith's theology of economics, self-interest is the central motive of human behaviour, even in religion. He tries to shed light on the religious institutions and the religious behaviour of his time through the prism of self-interest. Self-interest is at the centre of Adam Smith's analysis of religion.

Anderson argues that Adam Smith is the first economic imperialist who extends economic analysis to religion, so the economic imperialism of the recent research applying rational choice theory beyond traditional economic areas is not new.[66] In contrast to Anderson's argument, Leathers and Raines suggest that Adam Smith's theory of competitive religious markets is problematic.[67] According to the argument, Adam Smith's explanation for competitive religious markets does not always seem to be rational. This apparent discrepancy between those two arguments does not seem to lie in whether Adam Smith's approach to religious behaviour is rational enough to warrant him being labelled the first economic imperialist, or in whether it is limited by his favour of the established Church of Scotland. Rather, the point could be in the missing of the theological dimension of Adam Smith's self-interest in both arguments as Oslington properly points out.[68] Then the question is: is there any theological reason for him to assume that self-interest is still the strongest motive of religious behaviour and the foundation of the development of the religious institutions?

Adam Smith's seemingly uneasy attitude toward the Roman Catholic religion is shown in his arguments. Religious institutions and their clergies are described as pursuing their interest.[69] The seemingly hostile attitude toward religious institutions is more clearly shown in his argument that the constitution of the church of Rome is nothing but an immense and well-built fabric against 'the authority and security of civil government, as well as against liberty, reason and happiness of humankind, which can flourish only where civil government is able to protect them'.[70] Then, religion seems to be nothing but 'the grossest delusions of superstition'. However, Adam Smith's criticism is actually not against religion itself but against the poison

66 Gary Anderson, 'Mr Smith and the Preachers: The Economics of Religion in the Wealth of Nations', *Journal of Political Economy*, 961988), 1066–1088. 1086.

67 Charles G. Leathers and J. Patrick Raines, 'Adam Smith on Competitive Religious Markets', *History of Political Economy*, 24/2 (1992), 499–513. 512–513.

68 Paul Oslington, *Economics and Religion* (Cheltenham, UK ; Northhampton, MA: Edward Elgar Pub., 2003) 2 v. Vol. I Introduction.

69 WN V.i.g.17.

70 WN V.i.g.24.

of superstition and fanatic enthusiasm.[71] In his thought, religious superstition and enthusiasm are nothing but the poisons of the established church and their clergies pursuing their interest. In addition, it is natural for him to argue that the duty of an institution is in protecting every member of society from injustice or oppression carried out by any other member of society, and it is to be achieved not by human wisdom or knowledge but by leaving every human perfectly free as long as he or she does not violate the law of justice.[72]

This precise line of his thought is then applied to the religious institution. He criticizes any civil or religious organization which is against the natural efforts of every individual to better one's own condition. The point to be noticed in his argument is not in whether civil or religious institutions are necessary to intervene in human folly and injustice but in whether such institutions facilitate pursuit of one's own interest. No civil or religious institution stands against the natural desire of self-interest endowed by God's providence. Self-interest is the great antidote to the poisons of superstition and fanatic enthusiasm no matter whether they are at an institutional level or an individual level.[73] The constitution of the Church of Rome, delusions of superstition supported by private interest, cannot be overthrown by human reason; rather, the providential dimension of self-interest, Adam Smith believes, makes it possible. In his thought, it was not by the feeble efforts of human reason and virtue but by the natural course of things that such an immense fabric of superstitious delusion was weakened, partly destroyed, and would be likely to crumble into ruins altogether. Self-interest is again at the centre of his analysis of religion.

He emphasizes not only human weakness but also its providential nature. His argument is not simply that religion should be pure and rational. Rather, the point is that self-interest is given a priority so that it discovers its own way out of such absurdity and superstition. He does not have in mind another human institution to replace the previous institutions; rather, self-interest needs to be free in order for God to work through it.

71 WN V.i.g.14.
72 WN IV.ix.51.
73 WN V.i.g.25.

Superstition will be overcome not by the wisdom or virtue of humans but by the natural course of things.[74] At the core of his whole argument, there is always his faith in the role of self-interest which is the strongest motive of human desire inherent in God's providence as a natural way of salvation for individuals and society in the present and future. Adam Smith believes that by pursing our own interest, we promote the wealth of the society more effectually by an invisible hand than when we attempt to directly influence social welfare.[75] This again applies to the religious institutions. His self-interest is a religious faith in God's providence whose dimension is beyond economic or moral criticism. From this vantage point of his own view of self-interest, he tries to analyze the inner structure of the religious organizations, criticizes their delusions of self-love, describes their limits and possibilities, and predicts their future.

Adam Smith has a faith in the goodness of God. Even though the theological terms employed such as grace, repentance, the Cross, salvation, and revelation are rarely used in his approach to religious behaviour, the fundamental Christian faith is clearly shown in his works: humans are created in the image of God and destined for a life of eternal fellowship with God the Creator.[76] His religious idea is shown in his argument that an established church should produce all the good effects such as the uniformity of faith, the fervour of devotion, the spirit of order, regularity, and austere morals in the great body of the people, and he believes that they are achievable as shown even in the poorly endowed churches of Scotland and Switzerland.[77] His criticism against religious superstition and fanatic enthusiasm does not necessarily mean that he is a deist, or heretical against orthodox Christianity. In conclusion, Adam Smith's self-interest is the central motive even in human religious behaviour. He believes that the way to find an exit out of the contradiction between traditional church organizations and individual faith is in the providential nature of human self-interest. The theological dimension of self-interest is essential to understand Adam Smith's analysis of religious behaviour.

74 WN V.i.g.24.
75 WN IV.ii.9.
76 TMS III.ii.31.
77 WN V.i.g.41.

2.5. Summary and Conclusion

Economics is theological in Adam Smith's thought because his economic thoughts are built on his own theological foundations. In Adam Smith's theology of economic life, there is a transcendent and benevolent God who works through an invisible hand with providence and design for the harmony and benefit of humankind. Humans are created with an innate nature of self-interest by the providence of God the Creator, whose goodness never fails tending to the prosperity and perfection of the whole. His economic thought is founded on his theological faith.

Theology also has an economic aspect in Adam Smith's thought because his theological ideas are based on human self-conscious desire. Adam Smith's idea of self-interest is essentially *natural* in the sense that it consists of original and immediate instincts rather than the slow and uncertain determinations of our reason, and fundamentally *given* in the sense that it is endowed by Nature rather than acquired by human wisdom. He believes that the self-interest of bettering one's condition for happiness is natural and providential. It is natural as it is embedded in human instinct by Mother Nature, and it is providential as it is given by the wisdom of God who knows human weakness. His theological ideas are closely related to human self-conscious desire. Theological flavour is permeated in his economic ideas, and vice versa.

In conclusion, we may learn from his theology of economics the fact that human self-conscious desire is neither sin nor disobedience, but a gift from God. The human self-conscious desire is the stepping stone for salvation as it is not only economic rationality, but also has moral and theological dimensions. This illumination of the nature of self-interest gives us a new perspective about the division of economics and theology today. Self-interest is like a prism which shows various colours depending on which position we take. It has a broad range of meanings from rational self-consciousness to blind selfishness. The various colours of self-interest are sometimes the reason why there are difficulties and misunderstandings in the dialogue between economics and theology.

CHAPTER 3

Hegel's Rational Self-consciousness as a Way of Salvation

3.1. Introduction: The Aim and Scope of Discussion

The economic and theological landscape we see in Hegel's theology of economic life is quite different from Adam Smith's. The main concern of this chapter is to discover the possible relationship between economics and theology by paying close attention to the theological foundations presumed and embedded in his economic ideas. Thus, theological discussions are limited to the points that could be helpful for the book to illuminate the possible theological foundations embedded in his economic ideas, especially in comparison with Adam Smith's theology of economics. What is the hidden relationship between economics and theology in his thought, if any? That is the main question of this chapter. To explore some answers, salvation and human self-conscious desire are again used in this chapter as the conceptual tools with which to analyze his beautiful yet sometimes circular and ambiguous thought.

3.2. Hegel's Self-interest and Original Sin

Interestingly, Hegel's approach to self-interest is quite contrasting to Adam Smith's in spite of its similarity in some ways. An illumination of the theological reasons for the difference and similarity between them could offer significant clues with which to explore the relationship between economics and theology in Hegel. Original sin is one of the potential clues as it has an important role in his theological approach to economic life. This section deals with how the theological idea of original sin is related to his analysis of economic life based on self-interest.

Hegel's Self-interest and Inherent Nature (Ansich)

Humans are self-conscious beings. We all have self-conscious desire. We are aware of ourselves without knowing where the self-awareness comes from or how it is acquired. In a sense, it may be true that all living things with life in the world are self-conscious whether they are plants, insects, or animals, let alone humans including children. Self-awareness is a desire which may be an instinct given by the 'Wisdom of the Creator,' or an ability to be acquired by effort. Hegel divides this desire into two categories: one is the laws of nature; the other, the laws of right.[1]

Close attention needs to be paid to Hegel's use of the concept of nature and reason. He uses those concepts very sophistically to convey his own dialectical ideas. In his thoughts, the laws of nature are applied to all beings in the natural world, and the laws of right are related only to humans with rational[2] ability. Therefore, for him, children and uneducated humans become under the laws of nature.[3] There is a clear demarcation between natural instinct and rational ability. Namely, in Hegel's expression, self-interest seems to be a natural self-awareness under the laws of nature;

1 Georg Wilhelm Friedrich Hegel, Allen W. Wood, and Hugh Barr Nisbet, *Elements of the Philosophy of Right* (New York: Cambridge University Press, 1991), 13. Edited by Allen W. Wood; translated by H.B. Nisbet. Translation of *Grundlinien der Philosophie des Rechts, 1821.*

2 In this chapter, the words of 'reason' or 'rational' are always related to Hegel's *Vernunft* otherwise mentioned, which is normally translated into 'reason', not *Verstand*, which is generally translated into 'understanding'. Please refer to *A Hegel Dictionary* (Michael Inwood, 1993) for more. This does not necessarily mean that I agree with Hegel's classification.

3 PR 139.

self-consciousness is a rational self-awareness under the laws of right. This clarification is much more important than it seems. We can see how he uses these languages to create and play his own complex music in the world of his thought. If we accept his expressions and follow his logic, then there seems to be no exit out of his circular world. It is therefore necessary to know how to get in and out of his world to comprehend and enjoy his rich thoughts. The turning point of his circular arguments in his theology of economic life is the relationship between natural self-interest and rational self-consciousness. If self-consciousness is a way to get into his logical world, then self-interest is a way to get out of his circular world. He uses natural self-interest in a negative sense while rational self-consciousness is used in a positive sense in his theology of economic life. It is Hegel's favourite approach to divide one idea into two contradictory categories and then unite them again into a higher one, which is not only the strength, but also the weakness in his logic. The purpose of this section is to develop an idea of why he uses the human self-conscious desire of self-interest in the negative sense, examining whether there is any theological reason.

Hegel's approach to self-interest is narrow, compared to Adam Smith whose self-interest has a rich implication of economic rationality, moral sympathy, and theological faith. Hegel regards self-interest as selfish nature to be replaced with ethical life. This negative approach to self-interest is frequently shown when he mentions self-interest: a claim on mere formal right as selfishness;[4] selfishness as ethical degradation;[5] selfishness of enjoyment and comfort of one's particular needs as the ignorance of the nature of spirit and the end of reason;[6] self-interest as a sort of emotion, intuition, and opinion, which needs to be replaced with the establishment of right as law.[7] Then Hegel's thought about the motive of economic human behaviour seems to be quite opposite to that of Adam Smith who does not hesitate to give full rein to self-interest without any reservation. For

4 PR 37 Addition.
5 PR 179.
6 PR 187.
7 PR 211 Addition.

Hegel, self-interest is basically selfishness to be overcome. In addition, a more important point to remember in those negative expressions is that Hegel identifies self-interest as particular need, ignorance, emotion, intuition and opinion.

Then the next question to be addressed is whether or not Hegel's use of self-interest as natural selfishness is on the right track. Of course, it may be a matter of definition and even a language game; however, it cannot be so simply ignored, because there are theological preconceptions in its usage. As mentioned above, Hegel identifies self-interest with natural desires such as emotion, opinion, and ignorance, contrasting with rational reason such as ethics, spirit, and law, etc. These arguments are closely related to his own theological interpretation of human nature or instinct. Only rational humans, according to him, are able to tell the difference between good and evil, which are originally interpenetrated to each other from the beginning of the creation rather than evil is attached later to good from outside by God's passive permission.[8] From this theological assumption, he is therefore able to argue that we are free and self-conscious to overcome the duality of evil and good since humans are like God in their knowledge of good and evil. Human likeness to God cannot be in *natural self-interest* which is to be *naturally given* but in *rational self-consciousness* which is to be *consciously achieved*. In brief, we may recognize that his approach to self-interest is founded on his theological interpretation of human nature.

Original Sin and Human Natural Instinct

There is another theological precept in Hegel's approach to the natural instinct, which seems to be more fundamental in understanding his theology of economic life. That is the idea of original sin. The human desire for self-interest is closely related to his own theological interpretation of original sin. He believes that Christianity is better than other religions because it is based on the doctrine that man is by nature evil. That is original sin. He says that 'when he exists in an immediate and uncivilized condition, he

8 PR 139 Addition.

is therefore in a situation in which he ought not to be, and from which he must liberate himself. This is the meaning of the doctrine of original sin, without which Christianity would not be the religion of freedom'.[9]

Original sin is an ambiguous but important issue in theology. Even in Christian theology, there are various arguments regarding the meaning of original sin. Discussion about the theological meaning of original sin is not the main concern in this section. However, the matter of sin is important, because it is often discussed in relation to the scarcity of resources in economics. In this sense, Hegel's approach to self-interest is in essence theological because the biblical concept of original sin is a theological foundation of his economic thoughts. Hegel believes that self-interest as a natural instinct is related to the original sin of humans. Nature, in his thoughts, is evil to be overcome by human reason. According to him, humans are born with natural instinct that should be controlled by reason. He believes that the natural desire of self-interest is nothing but original sin. Hegel's economic approach to self-interest is essentially theological as it is related to original sin. In Hegel's thoughts, human nature is evil unless it is cultivated by the development of self-consciousness through ethical life. Nature is bad and reason is good. The human desire of self-interest is a natural instinct, so it is an evil to be overcome in civil society. For Hegel, the economic desire of self-interest as a natural instinct is related to original sin.

Hegel's self-interest is a human consciousness embedded in human nature like Adam Smith who puts self-interest at the centre of motivating power for human relationships in the market. However, in Hegel's thought, the desire of self-interest is an evil to be overcome because it is the natural instinct of humans. In Hegel's theological paradigms, humans are created to be able to choose between good and evil. Hegel's attitude towards the role of human self-interest for social welfare is dialectical as he believes that self-interest is a natural desire that should be preserved in the market for individuals to maximise their own interest, yet it should also be overcome by an ethical life in the state. The seeming contradiction in Hegel's understanding of the role of self-interest for human happiness is related to his theological preconception that the human desire of self-interest is based on

9 PR 18 Addition, italics mine.

human nature which is bad in essence. According to his own theological interpretation of original sin in the biblical story, he presumes that human desire of self-interest is a natural instinct to be overcome by rational self-consciousness. The natural instinct of self-interest in Hegel's economic thoughts is founded on an essentially theological presumption.

Hegel's idea about the relationship between individual self-interest and communal welfare is not properly understood unless we take into account his theological reason of why he believes that self-interest is natural rather than rational. The point to be made in this section is that his own theological preconception is the base of his economic ideas. There are theological foundations in his economic thoughts. His argument that economic self-interest should be under the control of rational reason is based on his own theological preconceptions, which are open to many questions from the perspective of theology of economics.

A further theological flavour of his solution can be noticed in his presumption that evil and good are interpenetrated to each other just as the body and soul are interrelated in human reality. This relationship between good and evil is also frequently shown in the passages of the Bible. For example, the Saint Paul says that "what I do is not the good I want to do; no, the evil I do not want to do" (Romans 7:19). This confession is exactly reminiscent of Hegel's approach where good and evil are inseparable; we are humans because we should choose between them; otherwise, we are not different from animals confined to their inherent nature; the meaning of original sin is not to be understood as coming from outside. If God, he argues, is the absolute positive in the creation of the world, it is impossible for us to find the negative in the world. According to Hegel, it is not a rational interpretation of original sin to believe that God is passively related to evil by his permitting the evil to exist. His solution is that the religious myth of original sin is to be rationally understood only when both the negative and the positive springs from the same root. According to him, it is because we can tell the difference between good and evil that we can be good.[10]

10 PR 139 Addition.

Therefore, according to Hegel, ethical life (*Sittlichkeit*) is to overcome this mere one-sided abstraction of self-certainty by rational self-consciousness of mutual recognition between evil and good. From this ethical approach to the meaning of original sin, Hegel faces the never-ending question regarding the relationship between fact and value, nature and spirit, faith and knowledge, and evil and good with rational self-consciousness. For Hegel, falling into the level of a personal feeling is nothing but an abstractive imagination far away from reality. He does not want to explain away the tension between good and evil by saying that truth itself cannot be known like Kant. For Hegel, truth is not in the individual's heart, emotion and enthusiasm.[11] His bold argument that evil and good is indivisible is the result of his rational (*vernunft*) explanation of the religious myth of original sin as he believes that self-consciousness knows how to discover a positive aspect in its own end.[12] His strong faith in the rational ability of human self-consciousness seems to come from his theological interpretation of original sin. He assumes that good and evil are indivisible just as God is both the absolute positive and the absolute negative at the same time. God's goodness never fails in Adam Smith's theology of economics; however, Hegel's God is neither good nor evil. His theology is different from Adam Smith's. This theological difference may lead to a different approach to the human economic behaviour motivated by the desire of self-interest. In Hegel's theological foundations of economic thoughts, economic behaviour based on natural self-interest has an origin of evil in itself and should be overcome by rational self-consciousness. Hegel's approach to natural self-interest in relation to original sin has not only an economic implication but also a theological meaning. We may conclude that his economic ideas are closely related to his theological assumptions.

There is a theological implication in Hegel's approach to self-interest. His idea regarding the role of self-interest is negative as far as salvation is concerned, compared to Adam Smith's positive approach to self-interest as a way of salvation. If natural self-interest is an evil to be overcome for

11 PR Preface, p. 15.
12 PR 140.

true freedom, then salvation is a matter of self-realization through the development of self-consciousness. To recognize the rose in the present is not something to be given by natural self-interest but to be achieved by rational self-consciousness in his thought. Consequently, his understanding of salvation seems to be narrow in its scope compared to Adam Smith's.

We may properly assume that religious salvation is a matter of deliverance and freedom from evil. According to Hegel, however, evil and good are indivisible as they are interpenetrated at the creation of the world in his interpretation of original sin; we are created in the image of God in our knowledge of good and evil; we are able to choose between good and evil; salvation from evil is not to be given naturally but to be achieved by our rationally self-conscious will. Accordingly, in Hegel's thoughts, salvation may be inevitably limited to individuals or groups with rational self-consciousness. In addition, as a natural conclusion of his argument, this world is only for individuals and groups who have self-conscious spirit; therefore, children, women, some ethnic groups and all other lives in this world may be lost and forgotten from God's economy.[13] In God's economy of salvation, however, the whole of creation including children, women, other ethnic groups, things on earth, and things in heaven are all to be reconciled with God (Colossians 1:20, Romans 8:22). This is one of the problems we need to take into consideration when we follow his differentiation between a negative concept of self-interest and a positive concept of self-consciousness.

His language of self-interest is one of his conceptual tools to describe human desire, so it may not be a matter of right or wrong. However, it needs to be taken into consideration that his negative attitude to self-interest as selfishness has its origin in his own theological interpretation of original sin, and that his theological interpretation does not seem to be on the same line with the biblical truth regarding sin and salvation. This tension or conflict is dealt with in his unique idea of the civil society where the power of natural self-interest as an economic motive in the market is not only affirmed but also negated for a higher level of self-consciousness.

13 PR 139 Addition; PR 166.

3.3. Hegel's Self-interest and the Civil Society

In the previous section, it is shown that the negative approach to self-interest has a theological background in Hegel's thought. The tension between self-interest and social welfare from a religious or theological perspective is not the issue related only to philosophers and theologians. The moral and religious backgrounds of the negative approach to self-interest can be seen among economists as well. In his *Essays in Persuasion*, Keynes, an economist, argues that self-interest is a necessary evil or sin, which may lead us out of economic necessity into daylight.[14] The idea of self-interest as a necessary evil is also shown in Hegel's explanation of the civil society, which gives us a clear view of how he approaches the concept of self-interest. In Hegel's economic thought, self-interest is accepted as the central motivator for civil society. The natural instinct of self-interest in the civil society, however, is not only emphasized but also negated. It is the dynamic motive of human behaviour, but needs to be elevated into a higher level of rational self-consciousness. He introduces civil society to preserve the dynamics of self-interest and to overcome its demerits. His seemingly negative attitude against natural self-interest changes when he explains his ethical life as the unity of abstract right and subjective morality. He puts the civil society in the middle between two other moments of the ethical life, the family and the state, and assumes that the civil society is composed of the system of need, the administration, the police and the corporation.

In the civil society, he emphasizes the dynamics of the commercial market composed by individuals who live for their own happiness by maximising their self-interest without direct consideration of others' welfare. He accepts that his contemporary society has developed to the stage where humans' self-interested autonomy cannot be negated by any reason. But he manages to put self-seeking desire at a proper place within his ethical thoughts without weakening its dynamics of human motive in spite of his generally negative approach to natural self-interest. The civil society is

14 John Maynard Keynes, *Essays in Persuasion* (London: Macmillan, 1931), 372–373.

Hegel's way of finding an answer to the difficult question of how to accommodate self-interest without losing its dynamics or causing a contradiction to his ethical system.[15] Hegel argues that interest groups help to mitigate the negative side of individual self-interest and learn the importance of living together in community. The unity between individual self-autonomy and social integration, in Hegel's thoughts, can be and should be preserved through the development of self-consciousness in the civil society.

However, this unity is still far away from an answer to the question about his differentiation between self-interest and self-consciousness because the role of unions or groups for the harmony between individual-interest and group-interest in the civil society is not yet free from self-interest. The unity is based on interest; a group-interest in this case, which can still be explained by the natural self-interest of individuals. Hegel also accepts the weakness of the foundation of the corporation; however, he brings in the role of the rational state as the final moment of the ethical life rather than return to the natural self-interest.[16] In Hegel's economic thoughts, unconscious behaviour based on natural self-interest is not reliable as a way for salvation, which is to be realized in the world by self-conscious rationality. Self-interest in relation to original sin is therefore not a proper tool for Hegel to explain the ethical dimension of human behaviour in the civil society. This rational (*vernunftig*) approach to human self-conscious desire is well summarised in his expression that we are at home in the world when we know it, and even more so when we have comprehended it (PR 4).[17] In Hegel's thoughts, the wisdom of God in nature has no meaning at all unless we are self-conscious of it.[18] His preference of rational self-consciousness to that of natural self-interest is related to his theological precepts: original sin, inseparableness of good and evil,[19] the state as the self-conscious Idea[20] and God as the self-conscious Idea.[21]

15 PR 253.
16 PR 254 Addition.
17 PR4.
18 PR 272.
19 PR 139 Addition.
20 PR 258.
21 PR 270.

In addition, his effort to integrate the positive and negative side of self-interest may give a clue to why his economic ideas are not only acclaimed but also criticized in various spectrums of thoughts such as liberalism, conservatism, socialism, and communism. As in his frequently quoted expression that the rational is real and the real is rational,[22] the circularity of his complex ideas is confirmed again in his argument of the negating and affirming of self-interest simultaneously and putting the private self-seeking into his system of ethical life not by just attaching but by placing it at the centre without diminishing either side of human behaviour. The reasons why he uses self-consciousness in explaining the motive of human behaviour rather than self-interest is probably because self-consciousness seems to be a convenient term for him to convey his circular and complex thoughts as it can be used in a broader sense than self-interest.

In sum, Hegel's language of self-interest has both a negative and positive implication. He does not simply nullify selfish desire as an obstacle against the self-realization of individuals in the ethical life of the community; rather, he tries to keep its momentum and transcend its selfishness without losing its powerful dynamics in the civil society. This may be one of the reasons why he prefers to use the language of self-consciousness in his works. Hegel tries to transcend a natural desire of self-interest by rational self-consciousness without losing the dynamics embedded in the desire of self-interest. We need to pay attention to how he uses self-consciousness to develop his economic, moral, and theological ideas, which is the issue to be dealt with in the following section.

3.4. Hegel's Self-consciousness (*Selbstbewusstsein*)

Hegel's self-consciousness is as colourful as Adam Smith's self-interest as it has different colours in it depending on how we approach it. At the centre of the human desire and will for salvation, there is an endless human motive

22 PR preface p. 20.

of bettering one's condition, which is self-consciousness in Hegel's language. Hegel believes that a natural human being has to be cultivated into a rational being by the development of self-consciousness in civil society. He uses an expression of self-consciousness rather than self-interest in his works to convey his ideas. If Hegel's salvation is not an event but a progressive process where individual self-consciousness is developed and unified with the level of self-consciousness of the ethical state and the self-realization of God in the world, then self-consciousness rather than self-interest is a more convenient conceptual tool to support his argument. Hegel's self-consciousness is analyzed into economic, ethical, and theological dimensions as preparation for the comparison with Adam Smith's self-interest in the following chapters.

Economic Dimension of Self-consciousness

Hegel's self-consciousness has an economic dimension. His idea of self-consciousness is the main motive driving the civil society where men try to maximise their own wealth by the single-minded pursuit of self-interest. Humans are in essence self-conscious beings in desire of economic salvation in his theology of economics.

An economic human is one who is able to achieve with self-autonomous rationality an economic salvation by maximising one's own self-interest. Hegel also fully accepts the important role of the dynamics of self-interest in the civil society as he believes that a human has self-consciousness in the system of needs, a commercial market.[23] In modern economics, a human being is described as an economic human who is free to maximise his own satisfaction by economic rationality. Such an economic human is surely self-conscious as he has freedom to act independently in pursuit of self-interest. This self-conscious motive of the modern economic human is shown in Hegel's understanding of the economic motive of individuals in the civil society where they are believed to be private persons who pursue their own interest.[24]

23 PR 189–208.
24 PR 187.

Then Hegel's self-consciousness has an economic dimension in the sense that self-seeking desire is fully accepted and recognized in his system of needs in which we are self-conscious individuals with freedom, self-autonomy, and desire of self-interest without care for others. In spite of the arbitrary will of the individuals, according to Hegel, the economic self-consciousness of individuals in the system of needs has an equilibrium similar to the planetary system whose laws are recognized in seemingly irregular movements.[25] Individuals with economic self-consciousness earn, produce and enjoy for their own happiness without noticing that they earn and produce for the enjoyment of others, which is resonant with the role of the invisible hand of Adam Smith.

Hegel's optimism with economic self-consciousness, however, does not continue. It is limited in the system of need, which is a part of the civil society. Evil and good are interpenetrated in his theological world, because he believes we are free in the sense that we are able to tell the difference between good and evil. In his theology of economics, the system of needs is necessary to preserve the dynamics of human desire, but it is far from being sufficient in itself as it is founded on natural self-interest that is to be transcended, rather than on rational self-consciousness that is to be achieved. He plays his own music that is permeated in his works, using his own theological preconceptions embedded in his economic thought. In addition, in Hegel's world, the laws of nature are to be replaced by the laws of right because the system of needs is not a destination but preparation to be transcended and preserved. Because of his theological belief that a human is like God in his knowledge of evil and good, he argues that we are able to bridge the two broken worlds of nature and spirit by the development of rational self-consciousness. In Hegel's thoughts, the economic self-consciousness is truly self-realized without losing the powerful dynamics of human autonomy and its communal value by the development of self-consciousness in the ethical life.

Of course, Hegel agrees that the mutual interdependent relationship created in the system of needs, the commercial market, turns natural self-interest into a contribution towards the satisfaction of the needs of everyone

25 PR 189 Addition.

else.[26] However, for Hegel, it is nothing but abstract right which is to be transcended and preserved into ethical life as the gap between self-interest and social interest cannot be bridged *naturally*. Therefore, from Hegel's perspective, the optimism in the explanation of the commercial market such as in Adam Smith is a one-sided abstraction that is far from a true description of the reality of the ethical life (PR 189). That is why he puts the civil society in the middle of the family and the state as a moment of the ethical life, and it is also why he puts the system of needs at the beginning of the civil society followed by the administration of justice,[27] the police and the corporation.[28]

In sum, Hegel fully accepts the concept of an economic human of mainstream economics. Individuals in the system of needs are men of self-interest, and all other things mean nothing to them; however, the economic self-consciousness is not the end but the beginning for ethical life through the development of self-consciousness.[29] In Hegel, economic self-consciousness has the dynamics of desire not as a final cause in itself but as an efficient cause for itself. It is not a destination but a preparation for ethical self-consciousness through the development of self-consciousness.

Ethical Dimension of Self-consciousness

Hegel's self-consciousness has an ethical (*sittliche*)[30] dimension. His idea of self-consciousness is ethical consciousness because it is related to his idea of reciprocal recognition (*Anerkennung*). Recognition is an ethical dimension

26 PR 199.
27 PR 209–229.
28 PR 230–256.
29 PR 182.
30 In Hegel's thought, *Sittlichkeit* (ethical life) is different from *Moralität* (morality). The former is related to customs and institutions of the community, and the latter is related to conscience and feeling of individuals. Refer to *A Hegel Dictionary* (Michael Inwood, 1993) for more details. In this chapter, 'ethical' means Hegel's *Sittlichkeit*, not his *Moralität*. However, this does not necessarily mean that I agree with this classification, which will be discussed in the following chapters.

of self-consciousness. Recognition itself is an important concept worth discussing in detail as in the works of Williams[31] and Honneth[32] to name a few. However, in this section, attention is limited to the relationship between self-consciousness and salvation in Hegel's theology of economic life. For Hegel, the moral dimension of human consciousness is not something to be given by a natural desire but is to be willed, known, and realized by the development of rational self-consciousness; self-consciousness finds its motive and base in ethics.[33] Hegel does not miss the importance of these human ethics in his concept of self-consciousness.

Ethics for him means more than morality based on personal self-certainty or conscience. In his ethical thoughts, we are not moral beings who can stay in our own self-certainty independently without recognition of others. Rather, we are ethical beings in need of mutual recognition; we cannot be ourselves without others' recognition of us, which cannot be possible without our recognition of them. Therefore, he argues that we have ethical self-consciousness which is in need of mutual recognition rather than a moral consciousness in which we are related to ourselves and ourselves alone.[34]

The first ethical moment of our self-consciousness is the family in Hegel's thought, followed by the civil society and the state. However, they are not separate stages. Rather, they are mutually related ethical moments with the state as the most advanced self-consciousness,[35] the end of history in his term, overarching the family which is based on the natural feeling of love[36] and the civil society which is based on self-interest.[37]

31 Robert R. Williams, *Hegel's Ethics of Recognition* (Berkeley: University of California Press, 1997).

32 Axel Honneth, 'Recognition and Moral Obligation', *Social Research*, 64/1 (Spring 1997), 16–35.

33 PR 142.

34 PR 135.

35 PR 257.

36 PR 199.

37 PR 182.

In addition, his introduction of the family as the first ethical life needs careful attention. There are two reasons for this. One is that ethical life is the essence of Hegel's thoughts. The family life is introduced as the first moment of ethical life followed by the civil society and the state. They are not three separate stages but interrelated moments as one; they cannot stand separately without the others. The other reason is that his introduction of the family life as the first moment of the ethical life seems to be intentional rather than accidental not only in its order, placing it as the first moment of the ethical life, but also in his use of language, using negative connotations such as nature and feeling. As argued in his *Science of Logic*, self-movement is, for him, nothing but the fact that something is itself and is also the negative of itself.[38] If self-consciousness is a self-movement in consciousness, then, following Hegel's logic, it is itself and is also the negative of itself. This logic is clearly shown in the family as the first moment of ethical life. His point is: the family is an ethical life with unity; however, the unity is based on the *natural feeling of love*, not self-conscious rationality.

According to Hegel, the first moment of the ethical life as mutual recognition is the family whose unity is based on the natural feeling of love, and we are not independent persons but members in the ethical life of the family.[39] The family, for him, is the first moment of the ethical life based on natural feeling of love. If we pay attention to the language used in his definition of the family, we can identify his use of the *natural feeling of love* introduced as the essence of the family. He assumes that our ethical self-consciousness as a member of the family is based on natural love. We might agree with his expression of natural love in defining the family as the first moment of ethical life. For Hegel, however, the expressions of nature and love are used in the context of his own thoughts. We remember that he differentiates the laws of nature and the laws of right in his preface of *Philosophy of Right*. In his thoughts, natural feeling belongs to the natural law and needs to be replaced with the social law. There is always a clear difference between natural feeling and rational reason in his thoughts.

38 Georg Wilhelm Friedrich Hegel and Arnold V. Miller, *Hegel's Science of Logic* (Atlantic Highlands, NJ: Humanities Press International, 1989). Translated by A.V. Miller; foreword by J.N. Findlay. Translation of *Wissenschaft der Logik*, 1816. Reprint. Originally published: London: Allen & Unwin, 1969.

39 PR 158.

If the feeling of love as the unity of the family is *natural*, then he can logically argue that the family as the first moment of the ethical life needs to be transcended and preserved in the following moment of the ethical life through the development of self-consciousness. If the natural feeling shared in the family is *love*, then he can again logically argue that the unity of the family is the ethical life in mutual recognition of others. He is able to put the family as the first moment of the ethical life only when he assumes that it is based on the natural feeling of love. Therefore, from a logical standpoint, he needs to argue that the family is a unity based on the natural feeling of love, where we are not independent, but members in the family with the unity of love although it is natural feeling.[40]

For Hegel, love is an emotional consciousness of unity with others. As long as love is a self-movement in consciousness, he is able to apply his logic to the feeling of love. According to him, love has two elements: self-negation and self-affirmation. In love, we no longer want to be self-sufficient persons because we would feel deficient and incomplete, so we want to recognize ourselves in others by whom we are recognized, just as they are in us. Love is the cause and result of this contradiction. The unity of the family is the ethical unity based on the natural resolution of the contradiction of love. We love each other in mutual recognition as a member of the family, which then is the ethical life based on natural feeling.

By defining the family as the first moment of the ethical life with the natural feeling of love, he seems to attempt to prepare a foundation on which the second moment of the ethical life is introduced. Love is a feeling, which is natural, but not rational in his thought; therefore, it cannot be real or actual for him. Natural self-consciousness as a feeling needs to be transcended and preserved into the following moment of the ethical life. The unity of family disintegrates naturally into a number of families as the children come of age, the sons become the heads of families and the daughters become wives.[41] They do not exist as members of the original family any more but as independent concrete persons related externally to one another. They lose the unity of the natural feeling of love but gain individual self-consciousness. The unity of the family is gone, and the differ-

40 PR 158 Addition.

41 PR 177.

ence of individuals becomes as the main sources of the ethical life, which he calls the civic society.[42] The *natural* self-consciousness of the unity in the ethical life of the family is to be transcended and preserved by the *economic* self-consciousness of the civil society. However, as we expect from his way of thought, the civil society itself is based on individual self-interest without communal unity, so it is not real, for it is not rational in his thoughts. The civil society is to be transcended and preserved again by the development of individual self-consciousness in the final moment of the ethical life; the state. In Hegel's thought, the civil society based on individual self-interest is required as the realm of difference mediated between the *natural unity* of the family and the *rational unity* of the state. However, we need to recognize that these three moments of ethics are not separate stages but three faces of one reality which is in essence rational in Hegel's thoughts: the family is a natural unity; the civil society is an economic unity presupposing the state which is the rational and absolute unity.[43]

The feeling of love in the family is to be transcended through an economic self-interest and realized as the rational love in the state; the natural ethics of the family is transcended through the economic ethics and realized as the rational ethics in the state. Individual self-consciousness is to be developed through the three moments of the ethical life. It starts from the family, develops in the civil society, and realizes in the state. We are not able to be good or free from evil unless we become the citizens of the state. In this vein, Plant acknowledges that Hegel's ideas are influenced by Steuart's theory of the statesman, but he argues that there are two main differences between them: one is that the state's intervention has to be consistent with the modern sense of personal freedom and self-consciousness; the other one is that Hegel is concerned about the enervation of human capacities and powers accompanying the civil society.[44] Plant's argument is congruent with Hegel's argument that all individual characters, all talents, and all

42 PR 181.

43 PR 182.

44 Raymond Plant, 'Hegel and Political Economy I', *New Left Review*, 103 (May 1977a), 79–92. Raymond Plant, 'Hegel and Political Economy II', *New Left Review*, 104 (July 1977), 103–113.

accidents of birth and fortune, and the waves of all passions are let free and limited only by reason which shines through them.[45] Self-consciousness is to be developed from immediate sensitivity to self-awareness to a reciprocity of inter-personal relationships through participation in ethical and cultural life. Hegel's self-consciousness as an essential motive of human behaviour has an ethical dimension. This is one of the issues Plant raises against Althusser's view of the system of needs. Through the mutually independent cooperation of labour in the civil society, an economic human's self-seeking consciousness is converted into communal welfare.[46]

However, there is still an important question worth careful discussion regarding Hegel's approach. In Hegel's language, there is a consistently repeated variation of a kind of logical music composed by two clearly distinct but ambiguously united set of musical notes throughout the three moments of the ethical lives: one is self-interest shadowed under the clouds of the natural, and the other, self-consciousness shining under the sun of the rational. Hegel starts from and always comes back to these distinct but united concepts. The validity of Hegel's means of approach cannot be logically nullified or affirmed, in Hegel's logic, both the logic and the reality are one and the same. We cannot evaluate his economic and ethical ideas properly unless his theological ideas are taken into consideration, because his language of self-consciousness is in essence theological. His own theological preconception of evil and good is permeated throughout his all ideas.

Theological Dimension of Self-consciousness

Hegel's self-consciousness has a theological dimension because he thinks that the final moment of the development of self-consciousness is finally to be realized in the state, which 'consists in the march of God in the world'

45 PR 182 Addition.
46 PR 199.

in his thought.[47] In his thoughts, rational self-consciousness is good, but natural self-interest is evil, so nature needs to be cultivated by rational self-consciousness. He believes that God is the ultimate self-conscious being who is immanent in the state. If the state, as Hegel argues, is the absolute ethical life in which our self-consciousness is to be finally realized in relation to others by the self-actualization of God marching in the world, our self-consciousness is in essence theological in so much as the state is the march of God.

More importantly, in Hegel, theological self-consciousness is closely related to economic self-consciousness. This point is worth careful attention as it is a possible turning point. Civil society seems to be the centre of his ethical life, rather than the family or the state. Hegel, of course, explains the three moments of the ethical life in the order of the family, the civil society, and the state. The family is the beginning of the three moments of the ethical life, the civil society as mediation, and the state is the final moment. Hegel seems to concentrate on the state as the final moment of the ethical life that transcends and preserves the previous two moments; however, the significance of his ethical life lies less in the state but more in the civil society. The family is a beginning of the civil society, and the state is the end of the civil society.

If we put more significance on the final moment of the ethical life than on the mediating moment, then the role of the state is more easily accepted as a solution. However, if we put more importance on the mediating moment, then we will be more cautious about the role of the state. In my opinion, Hegel's position seems to be closer to the latter approach; otherwise, he does not leave the problem of poverty unsolved as a contradiction in his thoughts as he accepts that even the state as the final moment of the ethical life cannot solve it. In his thought, both individual autonomy and personal dignity cannot be sacrificed even by the state. As shortly mentioned before, Plant also seems to have in mind this aspect of Hegel's ideas when he suggests two differences between Hegel and Steuart about the role of the state in relation to the system of needs, although he argues

47 PR 258 Addition.

that Hegel's ideas about the role of the state is likely to have come from Steuart's theory of the statesman rather than from Adam Smith's theory. One difference is the matter of the sense of unity between individuals and the state. Hegel, according to Plant, tries to revive the dead in Steuart's state by rejecting any role of the state conflicting against a personal autonomy and an individual identity with the state as a citizen. The other difference pointed out by Plant as the difference from Steuart is the matter of Hegel's consideration of the enervation of human capacities caused by the weakness of social ties and the mechanic nature in the system of needs. In spite of Steuart's influence, according to Plant's arguments, Hegel's state is different from Steuart because both the social cohesion and the inner life of humans are the main concern for Hegel's approach to the state in relation to the system of needs. Therefore, we may say that Hegel seems to emphasize the significance of the civil society rather than that of the state, although the state is assumed as the final moment of the ethical lives.

In addition, if we take into consideration the theological aspect of Hegel's self-consciousness, we may have a broader view to see the seeming tension between the power of the system of needs and the role of the state in Hegel's thoughts. His economic or political ideas are in essence theological in the sense that he tries to theologise the commercial market in ethical life by assuming that God is the God of the world on earth. Therefore, we could say that the importance of Hegel's thought is in the relationship between God's self-actualization and human self-realization through the development of self-consciousness in the world rather than in the relationship between the system of needs of the commercial market and the role of state in the ethical life.

The civil society is the stage of difference mediating between the family and the state.[48] In other words, economic self-consciousness is the desire mediating between the natural self-consciousness of the family unity in a feeling of love and the absolute self-consciousness of the state unity in a rationality of reason. For Hegel, the mediation is not possible unless the civil society can be fully developed in the state without losing its dynamics of the

48 PR 182 Addition.

economic desire of individuals; therefore, economic self-consciousness of the civil society is to be fully developed without losing its dynamics in the absolute self-consciousness of the state by God's self-conscious realization. From his argument, we can conclude that theological self-consciousness is therefore the completion of the economic self-consciousness. It is because the economic dimension of self-consciousness is related to the theological aspect of self-consciousness that the civil society is related to the state.

In addition, a theological aspect of self-consciousness is also shown in his interpretation of original sin. The true and rational meaning of the biblical story is, for Hegel, that human likeness to God in his knowledge of good and evil is in our ability to tell the good from the evil. The ability is nothing but our rational reason.[49] His rationality as a human ability is theological in the sense that his preconception regarding good and evil has a theological colour. Hegel's language of rational self-consciousness is influenced by his own theological preconception of good and evil. Then we need to know what he means when he says that God is to be realized in the world through the development of the self-consciousness of individuals in relation to others.

3.5. Two Poles of Hegel's Self-consciousness: Reason and Providence

In Hegel's theology of economics, self-consciousness is a way of salvation for individuals and society as it is rational and providential. Self-consciousness is a human reason to be realized in God's providential self-realization in the world. Reason and providence are two main poles of Hegel's self-consciousness as a way of salvation for individuals and society. To see the clear picture of the theological foundations of the economic thoughts in Hegel's ideas, it may be useful to approach his ideas from a different perspective by

49 PR 139.

choosing two poles support his ideas: reason and providence. Few studies have examined the relationship between human reason and God's providence from the perspective of the theology of economic life except the issue of the cunning of reason (Taylor 1975; Davis 1989; Ullmann-Margalit 1997; Hollis 1987).

Human Reason (Vernunft)

Hollis says in his *The Cunning of Reason*, the concept of 'rational' is probably 'the key mystery term to be decoded as the problems of understanding social action emerge.'[50] He is partially right when he says that rationality is the expression of the self in a social world. However, the human self-conscious desire is more than this. It is the expression of the self not only in a social world, but also, more importantly, in a theological world. The problematic concept of 'rational' cannot be properly decoded without taking into account its theological aspect of human self-conscious desire.

Hegel's approach to reason is fundamentally theological. Hegel's reason (*Vernunft*) is one of two main poles supporting his theology of economic life, because he believes that rational (*vernunftig*) self-consciousness as a way of salvation is a rational (*vernunftig*) ability to be realized in the world, which is in a process of constant development by dialectical movement. In Hegel's thought, this world is a being in the process of development by retaining identity with itself in its otherness. Therefore, a static and intuitive understanding (*verstand*) such as natural instinct cannot be the way to salvation in this rational (*vernunftig*) world.

Hegel's self-consciousness as a way of salvation is human reason to be realized in the ethical life, rather than natural instinct to be given by the wisdom of the Nature. However, human rationality cannot stand alone without divine providence in Hegel's thoughts, for his reason or rationality as the synthesis of transcendence and conservation is essentially theologically originated. God is to be self-realized in the world through the

50 M. Hollis, *The Cunning of Reason* (Cambridge: Cambridge University Press, 1987), 10.

development of self-conscious reason. In Hegel, human reason and God's providence are two faces of one reality. In this book, more significance is given to the intertwinement between reason and providence to see the interrelation between economic ideas and their theological backgrounds in his thoughts.

God's Providence

Hegel himself hardly uses the language of providence in his *Philosophy of Right* except in a few cases when he explains world history,[51] compared to his *Philosophy of History* in which providence is clearly explained and emphasized with the use of the cunning of reason. This is because the main concern of his *Philosophy of Right* is in the explanation of ethical life as a member of the state, while his *Philosophy of History* is about the development of human self-consciousness in history. For him, human reason is not one-dimensional analysis or understanding but synthetic rationality which includes its negation of itself just as God has his own negation of himself.[52] This logic is from his own theological precepts which are permeated throughout his economic thoughts. In his *Philosophy of History*, Hegel argues that providence is realized through human reason, and human reason is realized in God's providence which presides over the world and sets even the passions to work for the final end.[53] In his theology of economics, human nature as a passion is irrational, but it is still the cunning of reason and works for the final end of history in God's providence.

In the preface of *The Philosophy of Right*, Hegel says that the task of philosophy is to comprehend what is. In his philosophy, what is rational is real, and what is real is rational (*vernunftig*);[54] therefore, he can argue

51 PR 324, 337, 343 Addition.

52 PR 139.

53 Georg Wilhelm Friedrich Hegel, *The Philosophy of History* (New York: Dover, 1956). With prefaces by Charles Hegel and the translator J. Sibree; and a new introd. by C.J. Friedrich. Translation of *Vorlesungen über die Philosophie der Geschichte*, 1837.

54 PR preface.

in his circular argument that the rational is the real, and that the real is the rational. By saying this, he presupposes God's rational immanence in the world. Otherwise, God cannot be real. If God is real, then there is no other way but to conclude that God is rational; if God is rational, he is real in the world; God's providence is immanent in the world through human reason in Hegel's thoughts. Hegel, therefore, tries to unify knowledge and faith with his own two poles: reason and providence.

By using reason (*vernunft*) in relation to providence, there are broader and richer colours in its meaning than generally understood. Reason is no longer divisive and analytic understanding, but it is comprehensive and synthetic since reason is rational self-consciousness through which God's providence is to be realized in the world. God's providence is to be realized in the world by working through human reason. Human reason is rational self-consciousness to be realized in relation to others in the state. The state is the final moment of the ethical life to be completed by the march of God who is immanent in the world.

Two Poles of Hegel's Self-consciousness

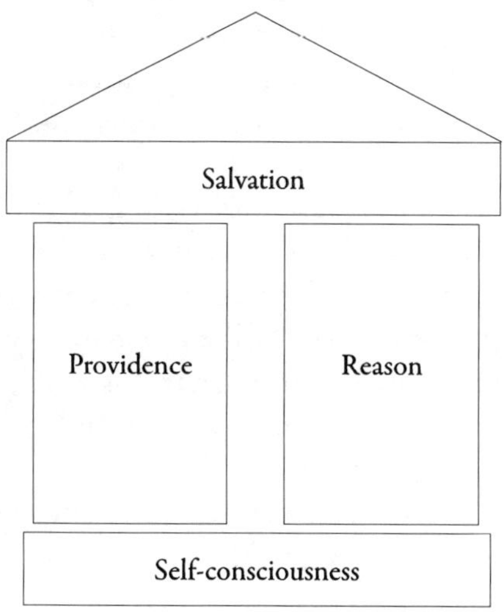

Self-consciousness is *a rational ability to be realised* in the divine state. God is to be actualised in the world through human self-realisation.

Both human reason (*vernunft*) and God's providence have their own negations in themselves in Hegel's logic. Both God and humans are self-conscious beings in Hegel's thoughts. Self-consciousness is to be realized only by self-negation in Hegel's logic. The momentum of self-negation and realizing self-consciousness is again recognition in Hegel's language, which has a similar role in the relationship with others as in Adam Smith's sympathy; however, the starting point is the direct opposite.

3.6. Self-consciousness as Human Reason to be Realized by God's Providence

Self-consciousness is a way of salvation for individuals and society in Hegel's theology of economics as he believes that self-consciousness is human reason (*vernunft*) to be realized by God's providence. The economic dimension of human desire for salvation is clearly shown in the ideas of Hegel, who also emphasizes the importance of an economic dimension of human beings through his acknowledgement of the importance of political economy, mentioning Adam Smith in *The Philosophy of Right* in his explanation of the civil society as a part of the ethical life. Although he consistently argues that a human is different from an animal, as an animal is limited to natural desires such as food and shelter, he does not underestimate the economic dimension of human life. Having property, for him, is an essential condition for us to live as people in this society as our self-consciousness is to be developed in mutual recognition with others through the rights of private property, which is essentially similar to the economic system of liberalism and different from the idea of communism.[55]

Hegel argues that we have two kinds of laws in our self-consciousness: the laws of nature which are simply there and the laws of right which

55 PR 52.

are derived by us.[56] By these seemingly conflicting messages in Hegel's argument, we may assume that an economic desire as a condition for salvation is more than just animal nature; it is preserved and transcended into a moral dimension by self-consciousness in Hegel's argument. An important point in Hegel's thoughts about economic desire, however, is that the laws of right are to be realized by us through the development of self-consciousness. In Hegel's thoughts, there is no consciousness of forgiveness in the laws of nature in which the highest truth is just in the existence of a law, while the spirit of reflection comes into play in the laws of right.

Hegel's ethical life is the realization of the idea of human good through the development of individual self-consciousness by mutual recognition in the society.[57] As we are essentially social beings, our negative freedom of being able to be free in ourselves is developed through individual self-consciousness into positive freedom of being able to be for ourselves.[58] Morality for Hegel is the higher stage of development of self-consciousness from its being-in-itself to its being-for-itself. By morality, we as a subject can see ourselves as an object in relation to others, which is the moral point of view for Hegel. However, forgiveness also has in it the same morality as what Hegel argues in *Philosophy of Right*. Human desire to be forgiven in the Lord's Prayer means that we are conscious of ourselves as objects to be forgiven.

However, Hegel goes further than this individual morality of self-certainty based on individual conscience in which there is, Hegel argues, still a possibility of tension between individuality and communality as our actions depend on our subjective and individual self-certainty with the external rule as an opposite. Such an individual morality as pure self-certainty melts away through the development of self-consciousness through mutual recognition to social morality: an ethical life. Only in this ethical life (*Sittlichkeit*), Hegel argues, is human freedom no longer in tension between I as an individual and I as a member of community. We consciously

56 PR preface.

57 PR 142.

58 PR 104, 105.

and knowingly accept the social rules for ourselves through self-conscious action in this ethical life (PR 142). This social dimension of morality of Hegel regarding humans as essentially social beings again seems to be exactly resonant with the point of forgiveness shown in the Lord's Prayer.

This is the reason why Hegel believes that Christianity is a religion of freedom. Christianity is a true religion, for Hegel, because Christianity liberates humans from the shackles of the evil of natural desire. Plant's historical approach to Hegel (1973) catches this mutually penetrated relationship between religious ideas and political economy in Hegel's works from a historical perspective.[59] However, there is no theological clarification about how theology and political economics are intertwined in Hegel's thoughts although he points out clearly that Hegel's metaphysical position is crucial in understanding his concern for political economy and its character.

Hegel's own argument starts with an analogy of body and soul from the very beginning of his *Philosophy of Right*, in which he explains his idea of right as the interpenetration between the metaphysical concept and its realization, just as our life is the unity of body and soul.[60] Hegel does not deny that body and soul may be separate; however, his analogy of body and soul means that our life is not possible without either one, for both are united and intertwined despite their separation. This idea seems to be extended again in his theology that God as spirit is one and the same as the God of the world. From this mystical vantage point, mystical as it is not still clear how it is separate and united, he argues against Adam Smith's political economics as an abstraction rather than a description of reality,[61] which is to be discussed in detail in a separate section after Hegel's theological position is clarified. We can at this stage see a glimpse of his theological background.

In Hegel, the harmony coming from the duet of nature as evil and spirit as good is a kind of musical tone flowing through all his thoughts via the development of rational (*vernunftig*) self-consciousness of individuals

59 Raymond Plant, *Hegel* (London: Allen and Unwin, 1973).

60 PR 1.

61 PR 189.

in the social world. By demythologising and philosophising the meaning of original sin from his own theological perspective, he argues that evil is the subjective self-consciousness confined in an abstract self-certainty or subjective self-satisfaction without social relation to others; the good is the realization of self-consciousness in the world which is the absolute and ultimate end of the world.[62]

From Hegel's point, conscience and morality (*moralität*) easily fall into evil rather than into good unless our self-consciousness has willingness to do our social duty of doing right to promote the welfare of both one's own and that of others.[63] Evil and good are indivisible in his thoughts, just as Hegel assumes that the human body and soul are interpenetrated.[64] Hegel continues to say that we can choose either evil or good; however, we cannot really be saved from evil unless we are rationally conscious of the evil of a moral hypocrisy confined in an abstract conscience. This rational self-consciousness (*vernunftig*) is his own interpretation of the meaning of human likeness to God in the knowledge of good and evil, which is for him a religious myth to be rationalized.[65] For Hegel, the rational self-consciousness may be an answer to the question of what to do in order to achieve eternal life.[66] Then salvation seems to be an ethical life (*Sittlichkeit*) matter in his thought as long as Hegel believes that human salvation is none of God's business but a matter of a human's self-realization through the development of rational self-consciousness in relation to others. However, his understanding of self-consciousness is essentially theological because the final moment of the ethical life is to be realized in the state which is for Hegel the march of God in the world.[67]

62 PR 129.
63 PR 134.
64 PR 1.
65 PR 139 Addition.
66 PR 134 Addition.
67 PR 258 Addition.

3.7. Hegel's Theology of Economics

Like many other modern economists, Hegel is also concerned about the conflict between private selfishness and communal welfare. Is there any solution to harmonize the powerful but selfish self-interest and the abstract but essential social welfare? This is one of the main issues he wants to tackle in his analysis of economic behaviour in the civil society as Adam Smith does in his *The Wealth of Nations*. However, in his economic thoughts, the economic self-consciousness in the market is not purely economic behaviour but essentially a part of the ethical (*Sittlichkeit*) life. In his ethical approach to the economic self-consciousness of humans, there are theological foundations. Hegel's economic thoughts cannot be properly evaluated unless his theological precepts are taken into consideration.

There are three main theological precepts we need to recognize in his theological foundations of economic thoughts: God, the world, and humankind. Firstly, God is assumed to be neither good nor bad, neither all-powerful nor all-knowing, but immanent in the world as a self-conscious being to be realized in the ethical (*Sittlichkeit*) community. If salvation is a matter of being with God, it is rational for Hegel to argue that our salvation is this worldly rather than other worldly as God is immanent in the world in his thoughts. Secondly, this world is the place where God is to be realized. If this world is the place of God's self-realization, it is rational for Hegel to argue that this world is eternal rather than transitory. Thirdly, humans have the will and freedom to be free from human natural instinct, original sin. If the natural instinct of humans is related to original sin, then it is rational for him to argue that human freedom and will are matters of rational ability rather than natural instinct. Hegel's economic thoughts are related to these theological foundations. Rational self-consciousness is a window through which we can see his complicated theological foundations of economic thoughts. Hegel believes that rational self-consciousness not only preserves the power of the human desire of pursuing one's own self-interest, but also overcomes the limit of human nature.

Hegel's God is a self-realizing spirit (*Geist*) in the world. There are many books and articles dealing with Hegel's approach to God. In his book *Hegel and Christian Theology*, Hodgson argues that there is a flavour of religious pluralism in Hegel's idea of God because God's self-realizing spirit is one-in-many and many-in-one, fracturing and mending the wholeness of God and world.[68] However, we can also feel a clear tension between good and evil, reason (*vernunft*) and nature. In Hegel's theological foundations of economic thoughts, God seems to be assumed to be neither good nor bad, neither all-powerful nor all-knowing, but immanent in the world as a self-conscious being to be realized in the ethical community. In Hegel's theology of economic life, we are self-conscious beings just as God is self-conscious Spirit (*Geist*). The question is: how does the idea of God affect his economic thought? Therefore, attention is paid to discovering the possible link connecting economic ideas and Hegel's God by strategically using the concepts of self-consciousness and salvation, rather than doing in-depth study about his doctrine of God.

If salvation is a matter of being with God who is to be realized in the world, our salvation is in this world rather than in the world to come. This world where God is to be realized cannot be transient any more, but it should be eternal. Human economic behaviour then has an important meaning in his theological foundation of economic thoughts. In addition, Hegel's God is a self-conscious rational being, so there is hope for us to grasp God in our knowledge. His frequently quoted circular expression about God is as follows: if God is real, then he is rational; if God is rational, then God is real. For Hegel, God is a self-conscious, rational, immanent being to be realized in the world. He believes that God is neither self-sufficient nor perfect, but needs to be realized in the world by the development of rational self-consciousness. In contrast to the otherworldly religious faith that salvation is to be free from this world on earth and to be with God in heaven, God's immanence in the world is the central idea in his theological foundations of economic thoughts. God's economy of

68 Peter Crafts Hodgson, *Hegel and Christian Theology: A Reading of the Lectures on the Philosophy of Religion* (Oxford: Oxford University Press, 2005), 283.

the world is human economy, and human economy of the world is God's economy in his theological foundations of economic thoughts. There is no clear demarcation between God and humans in his thought.

In sum, Hegel believes that salvation is to be united with God's self-consciousness through rational development of self-consciousness and that God as the absolute Spirit is to be realized on earth through the development of human self-consciousness rather than staying alone in heaven as an all-sufficient being. There is no clear distinction between humans and God in his thoughts. A human is a finite being in nature but an infinite being in union with God's self-consciousness. He therefore argues that the present is no longer just vanity, but that the important thing is to recognize the eternal, the immanent, and the present here and now from the appearance of seemingly transient and temporal things. A true philosopher who has the rational insight of reconciliation with reality recognizes reason as the rose in the cross of the present, and enjoys it. Here is the rose; therefore, dance here. In other words, in Hegel's thought, we can recognize the eternal, immanent, and present God in the transient and temporal experience of our daily lives.

3.8. Summary and Conclusion

In Hegel's theology of economics, a theological idea of original sin is linked with an economic idea of self-interest. Firstly, Hegel's understanding of self-interest is analyzed in relation to the concept of original sin that is traditionally one of the main issues in Christian theology. It is shown that self-interest is not just an economic matter but essentially a theological issue in Hegel's thought. His negative attitude against natural human desire cannot be properly explained without his own theological precepts embedded in his thought. Secondly, self-consciousness is chosen as a conceptual tool as there is a tension between nature as what is and reason as what ought to be in Hegel's thought. Self-consciousness is analyzed to show that it has economic, ethical, and theological dimensions. Thirdly, it is suggested that reason and providence are the two main poles of his understanding of self-consciousness. This chapter concludes that self-consciousness is a way of salvation in Hegel's thought as he believes that the dynamics of natural self-interest is to be preserved but overcome through the development of rational self-consciousness.

Hegel's economic ideas are theological thoughts. His analysis of economic activities is essentially theological as his ethical (*sittliche*) approach to human economic behaviour is permeated by his own theological preconceptions: God's self-realizing immanence in the state, natural self-interest in relation to original sin, and rational self-realization as a way of salvation in the world. In Hegel's theological foundations of economic thoughts, reason (*vernunft*) is good but nature is bad. There is a tension between nature as what is and reason (*vernunft*) as what ought to be, and he believes that this conflict needs to be solved by rational (*vernunftig*) self-consciousness. The dynamics of natural self-interest is to be preserved but overcome through the spirit of the divine state that is the God immanent in the world. Self-consciousness (*selbstbewusst*) is the focal point for salvation in his theology of economic life. In addition, economic salvation and theological salvation are not separate but intertwined in his thoughts. The economic instinct of maximizing self-interest is preserved in the market and overcome in the ethical life through the development of self-consciousness by internalising social interest as a member of the state.

In addition, Hegel's theological thought is basically economic as his theological approach to human behaviour is closely related to the development of human self-conscious desire. Salvation is something to be achieved in the world by rational (*vernunftig*) self-consciousness, which is a way of salvation for individuals and society. He believes that human self-consciousness of bettering one's condition for happiness is rational (*vernunftig*) and providential. It is rational (*vernunftig*) as it is a human ability to be free from the bondage of human natural instinct, and it is providential as it is to be achieved in the process of actualization of God in the world. Consequently, Hegel's thought is a proper place to discover the relationship between economics and theology and to confirm that economic ideas have theological foundations even though he himself might not have noticed the theological dimension of his own economic ideas and the economic aspect of his theological thoughts.

In conclusion, Hegel has a theologically different perspective from Adam Smith but leads to the same conclusion in terms of the role of self-consciousness as a way of salvation. Their similar but different understandings of human nature illuminate the complicated aspects of the world we live in, in general, and the relationship between economics and theology, in particular. Hegel's dialectical and sometimes circular analysis of human behaviour is closely related to his theological approach to self-interest. This leads us to the same conclusion that it is necessary to have a holistic approach to human behaviour.

CHAPTER 4

Sympathy and Recognition

Sympathy is Adam Smith's language of defining the relationship between individuals, while recognition is Hegel's term for when dealing with it. The aim of this chapter is to show that sympathy and recognition seem to be similar, but they are different to each other in many ways. The main reasons to be suggested are again their theological backgrounds imbedded in their economic ideas. By showing that sympathy and recognition are the moral and ethical dimensions of self-conscious desire in Adam Smith and Hegel respectively, it will be argued that their theological foundations affect their understanding of moral relationships among individuals. In addition, it will be shown that their understanding of love is also closely related to their sympathy and recognition. Finally, the dialectical aspects of human relationships will be discussed.

4.1. A Brief Comparison of Adam Smith's God and Hegel's God

If we can define theology as the systematic study of religious faith regarding humanity, the world, and God, theology may include economics not only because economics is the systematic study of human behaviour in the market, which is a part of the same world as in theology, but also because human self-consciousness could be the common platform on which economics and theology may have a dialogue. Theism, pantheism, and panentheism are the typical categories introduced in theology to clarify various approaches to God. The aim of this section is not in theological investigation of the doctrine of God, but in clarifying the role of theology in the economic thoughts of Adam Smith and Hegel.

Both Adam Smith and Hegel believe in God the creator. However, for Hegel, God is not a transcendent creator of the world but rather a Spirit permeating everything. God and the world are not separate but belong together.[1] Hegel's God who is to be realized in the world is different from Smith's God who presides over the world. In Hegel's thought, God is in everything, and everything is in God. His understanding of God, therefore, belongs to neither traditional theism nor pantheism, but rather to panentheism.[2] For Hegel, God comes to be himself in the end, when he realizes himself in the world through self-realization just as humans come to be themselves when they realizes themselves in relation to others. God is neither good nor bad; God has both the positive and the negative as well. We are created in likeness to God. We have the rational ability to tell good from evil although they are indivisible. This present world is not just a transient or passing moment, but the place where God's self-actualization is to be achieved. The tension inevitably caused by the synthesis between nature and reason is named as the cunning of reason in Hegel's thought, compared to Adam Smith's use of the invisible hand to explain the theological dimension of both self-interest and self-consciousness. For Adam Smith, however, God is the all powerful God, the Creator, and humans have natural weakness as the creature; the world is not God-forsaken as God the almighty is always good; self-interest is given to humans by the wisdom of God.

Interestingly, both of them accept and use the creation story of the Bible in their arguments. However, their respective understandings of its theological meaning are quite different to each other. They both have theological preconceptions overtly or covertly in their arguments without theological clarification. By analyzing these differences, we may illuminate the theological ideas permeated in their economic thoughts. For Hegel, the creation story is religious myth.[3] The rational meaning of the likeness

1 Clark H. Pinnock, *Tracking the Maze: Finding Our Way through Modern Theology from an Evangelical Perspective* (San Francisco, CA: Harper & Row, 1990), 103.

2 Stanley Grenz and Roger E. Olson, *20th-Century Theology: God and the World in a Transitional Age* (Downers Grove: InterVarsity Press, 1992), 39.

3 PR 139 Addition.

or image, for him, is that 'human is like God in his knowledge of good and evil.' Humans have the ability of differentiating good from evil. We can presume that this is one of his theological preconceptions or bases on which he builds his own understanding of human reason as a way of salvation for individuals and society. For Adam Smith, the creation story is related to his religious faith in the never-failing goodness of God, the Wisdom of Nature.[4] Adam Smith's self-interest is an efficient cause in the sense that it is not a final end. True salvation is not in this world but in a life to come. Hegel's self-consciousness is however a final cause in the sense that salvation is to be realized by the development of self-conscious rationality in the world.

For Adam Smith, God is transcendent over the world; God is a God of love as in Hegel; God does not leave the world uncared. Self-interest is the providential goodness of God; a human being is created with an instinct of self-interest which is not something to be achieved by human reason. However, Hegel actually uses self-consciousness rather than self-interest to explain that human consciousness is something to be developed by reason. Self-interest is, in Adam Smith's thought, a gift given by God who is the creator of the world and humankind, compared to Hegel for whom God as the creator is a myth to be demythologized by human reason; self-interest has its own way to the salvation by God's invisible hand. Therefore, self-interest is in essence theological.

For Adam Smith, God is the Creator; humankind and the world are created by the Wisdom of Nature from God's goodness. There is a clear division between the goodness of the Almighty God and the weakness of humans as created beings. The weakness of humans is an inherent attribute in the sense that a human is a limited being as creature, but it is not punishment or evil but grace in Adam Smith's thoughts. He has faith in the goodness of God, the Wisdom of Nature who never leaves humankind alone. His God is transcendent above the world, so it is natural for him to presume that the world is essentially transient because true happiness is only in a world to come.

4 TMS III.2.31.

For Hegel, however, God is immanent in the world, so it is rational for him to think that this world has an eternal nature because true freedom or salvation is to be achieved in the world by human self-consciousness to be realized in the state. Hegel's theology is penetrated into his ideas because he believes that God is to be realized in this world. Traditional bifurcation between God and humankind is to be overcome in his world of truth. Synthesis is good, and division is evil in Hegel's system of thought.

4.2. Adam Smith's Self-interest and Hegel's Self-consciousness

Adam Smith's self-interest and Hegel's self-consciousness are related to the same human consciousness but with different theological foundations. Adam Smith's self-interest is a natural consciousness, while Hegel's self-consciousness is a rational consciousness of humans. Adam Smith believes that self-interest is a way of salvation as it is natural in this world of Mother Nature. Hegel however believes that self-consciousness is a way of salvation as it is rational in this world of Reason. Adam Smith's self-interest is not human rational ability but human natural weakness to be given by the goodness of Wisdom of Nature, while Hegel's self-consciousness is not natural weakness but rational ability to be realized in the ethical life of the state as God's highest manifestation. Both Adam Smith's self-interest and Hegel's self-consciousness are respectively at the centre of the theological foundations of their economic thoughts. If God is a self-conscious being as we are, we may properly assume that a connecting point between God and us is self-consciousness for Hegel and self-interest for Adam Smith.

A bridge Connecting Economics and Theology

In Hegel, the connecting point between God and humans is self-consciousness; the meeting place is wholly in the world as God is the God of immanence in the world. God and humans are connected in ethical life through self-consciousness by mutual recognition. God does not stay in heaven in self-sufficiency but comes into the world for self-realization in the ethical life of the state while humans do not stay in nature in self-contingency but comes out to the world for self-realization in the ethical life of the civil society. God and humans are united by mutual self-realization in the ethical world, where theological self-consciousness is economic self-consciousness in ethical self-consciousness. Theological precepts are intermingled with economic ideas in his dialectical approach to rational self-consciousness.

In Adam Smith, the connecting point between God and humans is self-interest; the meeting place is partly in the world as God is the God of transcendence. God and humans are connected in the commercial market through self-interest by the Wisdom of God. God does stay in heaven in self-sufficiency but presides over the world with the Wisdom of Nature in the commercial life of the market. The Wisdom of Nature and humans are united by the goodness of God in the commercial world where theological self-interest is economic self-interest in moral self-interest. Theology and economics are united by natural self-interest which is essentially a natural desire to be given by God.

Theology is an abstract science dealing with the matter of human desire in religious behaviour while economics is a concrete science dealing with the matter of human desires in economic behaviour. How can they be related to each other? Hegel's answer would be that self-consciousness is a human desire to be completed in ethical relationships with others through recognition. Adam Smith's answer would be that self-interest is a human desire, an instinct innate in the natural relationship with others through sympathy.

Natural Self-interest and Rational Self-consciousness

Self-interest is a way of salvation for Adam Smith as it is the instinct embedded in human nature in his theology of economic life, while self-consciousness is a way of salvation for Hegel as it is the rational ability to be developed in the process of self-realization. Both Adam Smith and Hegel pay attention to the role of the human self-conscious desire as a way of salvation. However, their approaches are quite different to each other. The human self-conscious desire is something that is natural in Adam Smith and to be rational (*vernunftig*) in Hegel. Hegel's rational self-consciousness is something to be realized by development of self-consciousness in the state which is the highest manifestation of the immanent God, while Adam Smith's natural self-interest is something to be given by the wisdom of Nature.

There are theological backgrounds for this difference. In Adam Smith's theology of economic life, the human self-conscious desire is essentially good as it is given by God whose goodness never fails. However, for Hegel, it is a human ability to be realized by the development of rational self-consciousness in the world where God is also to be realized. The human self-conscious desire is in essence natural for Adam Smith, and rational (*vernunftig*) for Hegel. Adam Smith's self-interest is a natural instinct embedded in human nature, while Hegel's self-consciousness is a rational ability to be realized. Adam Smith believes that human nature is good as it comes from God's wisdom, so it cannot be negated by feeble human reason. Hegel believes that nature is evil as it is related to human weakness, so it needs to be negated by human rational (*vernunftig*) ability. Therefore, Hegel's self-consciousness is the human self-conscious desire *to be realized* by human freedom and will, while Adam Smith's self-interest is the human self-conscious desire *to be given* in human nature and instinct.

This bifurcation comes from three main differences in their theological foundations regarding God, humans and the world. Firstly, Adam Smith's God is all-powerful, all-knowing, always good, and presiding over the world. God exists even without the world. Hegel's God is however neither good nor bad, neither all-powerful nor all knowing, but to be realized in the world. Without the world, there is no God. Secondly, in Adam Smith's thought, humans are weak in their rational ability, but have a possibility of goodness in their natural instinct. However, in Hegel, humans are evil in their natural instinct, but have a possibility of development in their rational ability. At the centre of this bifurcation, there is a theological precept of original sin. The biblical concept of original sin has no place in Adam Smith's understanding of human beings, while it has the central role for Hegel. Thirdly, for Adam Smith, this world is transitory but full of God's providential goodness expressed in the invisible hand, while Hegel's world is real and eternal but in the process of self-realization with God's providence working through the cunning of reason. Consequently, Adam Smith's salvation is something to be given in a world to come, while Hegel's salvation is something to be achieved in this world.

In Adam Smith's theology of economic life, the self-conscious nature is good as it is given by God whose goodness never fails. The self-conscious desire is a gift from God, so the natural self-interest is a way of salvation for Adam Smith. Nature and providence are two main poles of his concept of self-interest. Hegel, however, believes that nature is an evil to be overcome as it is related to Original sin. Freedom and will are given by the immanent God who is also to be realized in the world through the ideal state. The self-conscious desire is embedded in human nature as original sin to be overcome by reason, so the rational self-consciousness is a way of salvation for individuals and society for Hegel. Reason and providence are the main poles of his self-consciousness. Both Adam Smith and Hegel believe that the self-conscious desire is a way of salvation for individuals and society. However, the human consciousness is natural instinct for Adam Smith, but rational reason for Hegel.

To be Given or to be Realized

Hegel's self-consciousness is something *to be realized* by human freedom and will, while Adam Smith's self-interest is something *to be given* in human nature and instinct. This delicate difference between these two important thinkers in approach towards the essential motive of human economic behaviour comes from their own anthropology and theology.

Hegel's self-consciousness is as colourful as Adam Smith's self-interest. Self-consciousness is desire.[5] Hegel's self-consciousness as desire, however,

5 Georg Wilhelm Friedrich Hegel, Arnold V. Miller, and J.N. Findlay, *Phenomenology of Spirit* (Oxford: Oxford University Press, 1977).

is not something to be given naturally as in Adam Smith's approach to self-interest which is an inherent instinct given by the Wisdom of God, but something to be realized rationally by reciprocity of interpersonal relationships through mutual recognition.

Adam Smith clearly criticises such human consciousness as blind selfishness. Self-interest for Adam Smith is neither morally degraded selfishness nor ethically neutral rationality; rather, it is an imbedded instinct in humans by God's providence. We may assume that one of the reasons why Hegel uses such a negative definition of an economic human in spite of his knowledge of Adam Smith's ideas is because of the necessity of differentiating his ethical life (*Sittlichkeit*) from individual morality. In Hegel's thought, individual morality based on one's own conscience and feeling is not the same as the ethical life which is related to the customs and institutions of the community to which individuals belong to.

For Hegel, self-consciousness (*selbstbewusst*) is not something to be given to humans naturally as laws of nature but something to be realized by humans as laws of right. This is his vantage point from which he develops his economic and ethical arguments. By using self-consciousness, Hegel fills the gap between emotional feeling and rational reason and connects the particularity of the family based on the feeling of love and the universality of the state based on the rationality of reason through the mediation of the civil society which is composed of self-conscious individuals whose ends are private, particular, and contingent.[6] Hegel's self-consciousness is to be realized, while Adam Smith's self interest is to be given.

6 PR 185.

4.3. Adam Smith's Sympathy and Hegel's Recognition (*Anerkennung*)

The difference between Adam Smith's self-interest as human nature and Hegel's self-consciousness as human reason is shown again as sympathy in Adam Smith's thought and recognition (*Anerkennung*) in Hegel's ideas. The reconciliation between individual interest and communal welfare is an important issue not only for Adam Smith but also for Hegel. Their approaches to the issue are different from each other because their theological world-views are different. Hegel's recognition (*Anerkennung*) is based on human reason (*vernunft*) while Adam Smith's sympathy is based on human nature. Recognition (*Anerkennung*) is rational consciousness to be achieved by human reason while sympathy is natural consciousness embedded in human nature. The moral relationship among individuals based on self-interest is sympathy in Adam Smith's language, while the ethical relationship among individuals based on self-consciousness is recognition in Hegel's expression. Adam Smith's sympathy is a moral principle of human relationships based on self-interest, and Hegel's recognition an ethical principle of human relationships based on self-consciousness. Adam Smith's sympathy is a natural relationship, while Hegel's recognition is a rational relationship. Adam Smith's sympathy is based on self-interest, whereas Hegel's recognition is on self-consciousness. Adam Smith's sympathy is the mutual relationship between individuals who act with the motive of self-interest, while Hegel's recognition is the mutual relationship between individuals who behave according to the motive of self-consciousness.

Adam Smith's Sympathy

Sympathy is the moral dimension of Adam Smith's self-interest. He believes that there is a moral principle in human nature. The important role of sympathy in approaching the human desire of self-interest is shown in his starting paragraph in the *Theory of Moral Sentiments.*[7] He begins his moral theory from the presumption of natural sympathy of ordinary people, not from such a moral virtue to be achieved by human reason. Sympathy and self-interest are mutually interrelated in the sense that they are natural human desires inherent in the human instinct given by God's providence. The theological dimension of his arguments shown in the natural sympathy based on self-interest is far from being ironic or ornamental, rather, it is the cradle in which his whole system is born into. Sympathy is a psychological tripod with emotionality, rationality, and faith.

'Do to others as you would have them do to you' (Luke 6:31). In this message summing up the main religious themes in the Bible, a dynamic relationship between self-interest and altruism is hidden. The message does not mean that we need to love others only when we want to be loved, nor does it mean that we do not need to love others if we do not want to be loved by them. The point it says is rather that the reason that we need to love others is that we all have the desire to be loved by others. We are required to and able to love others because we have natural interest in being loved. To be loved by others, we need to love them. Self-love is not something to be negated for others-love; rather, it is an essential motive or an efficient cause to love others. This biblical theme is repeated again in Smith's version of moral relationships, that is, sympathy. He tries to build up a foundation on which to overcome the traditional dichotomy between self-love as vice and others-love as virtue as he says that the most hardened violator of the laws of society is not altogether without sympathy. In this psychologically sympathetic process, self-interest has a central role in an action for others-interest rather than being negated as sinful desire. Whatever the meaning of the golden rule is, Smith would say that it is not possible for us to love others without the desire of self-interest. In Smith's thought, I love others because I have desire of being loved by others. Love is based on mutual sympathy to be activated only when we have a desire of self-interest in what we would have others do to us.[8]

7 TMS I.i.I.1.
8 TMS VII. ii.3.16.

In addition, self-love and others-love are mutually interrelated as two faces of one reality: self-interest. In Smith's arguments, the moral and emotional term of sympathy is substituted for love, the term coloured by religious flavour. By using sympathy, he may be able to overcome the tension between unstable passions and feeble virtue and discover a way of salvation for individuals and society in harmony, because sympathy is neither something to be acquired by human reason or virtue, nor something to be negated by human will and passions. Sympathy, for him, is a natural instinct like self-interest, which is inherent in humans and given by God.

According to Adam Smith's sympathy, a moral dimension of self-interest, we need to know how to love ourselves before loving others. We may love others because we love ourselves. Self-interest rather than self-negation is the central motive of human behaviour in his concept of sympathy. In Adam Smith's sympathy, I sympathise with you because I have interest in myself. Hegel's recognition is something to be achieved by mutually self-conscious individuals by reason, while sympathy is something to be given to individuals with self-interest by nature. Hegel would say we are able to recognize each other as we have rational self-consciousness to be realized by the highest ethical life of the state, while Adam Smith would say that we are able to sympathise with each other as we have natural self-interest given by the wisdom of Nature.

Hegel's Recognition (Anerkennung)

Hegel's recognition is an ethical (*sittliche*) dimension of self-consciousness regarding interpersonal relationships. As Honneth says, Hegel's approach to the interpersonal relationship is more than personal morality, because human self-consciousness is dependent on the experience of social recognition in the sense that a human is essentially a communal being.[9] In his book *Hegel's Ethics and Recognition*, Williams also argues that the theme of

9 Axel Honneth, 'Recognition and Moral Obligation', *Social Research*, 64/1 (Spring 1997), 20.

recognition is largely ignored in spite of the importance of its role in Hegel's thought.[10] However, a different approach to Hegel's recognition is taken in this section to compare to Adam Smith's sympathy. In the previous chapter, it is shown that Hegel's economic ideas have theological foundations, and self-consciousness is used as a conceptual tool to discern his theology of economic life. Hegel's negative attitude against natural self-interest is clearly shown again in his analysis of interpersonal relationships. That is the main point to be given attention.

Hegel believes that there is an ethical (*sittliche*) principle in human relationships. According to the ethical principle, we need to know how to love others before loving ourselves. We may love ourselves because we love others. Self-negation rather than self-interest is the central motive of human behaviour in his concept of recognition. In Hegel's recognition, I recognize myself in you, and yourself in me.[11] This reflective identification is shown again in his understanding of love in the first moment of ethical life, the family.[12] In his *Phenomenology of Spirit* (1977), Hegel explains the relationship between the master and the slave in his own dialectical logic.[13] A conscious being can be conscious of itself only in recognition of another conscious being. We require the recognition of others in order to recognize ourselves. This recognition is often asymmetric when one person is a servant, and the other is the master. This is an unstable relationship because the recognition of one's servant isn't worth much. The eventual resolution is for both to recognize the other as an equal. This recognition is both similar to and different from Adam Smith's sympathy. It is similar in the sense that they are relational. But it is also different, as our self-consciousness does not need other-consciousness in Adam Smith's self-interest; rather, we need our self-consciousness before we recognize others' self-consciousness. For Adam

10 Robert Williams, *Hegel's ethics of recognition* (Berkeley, CA: University of California Press, 1997).

11 PR 146–147.

12 PR 158.

13 G.W.F. Hegel, Arnold Miller and J.N. Findlay, *Phenomenology of Spirit* (Oxford: Oxford University Press, 1977), 111. Translated by A.V. Miller; with analysis of the text and foreword by J.N. Findlay. Translation of *Phänomenologie des Geistes*, 1807.

Smith, self-interest is more universal than Hegel assumes. Hegel believes that recognition of others is necessary for self-consciousness. Of course, we are conscious of others, but this does not necessarily mean that we need recognition of others for us to be self-conscious. Sympathy is that we are conscious of others as we are self-conscious, while recognition (*Anerkennung*) is that we are conscious of others so that we are to be self-conscious. In Adam Smith's sympathy, self-consciousness is a pre-condition for us to be able to be conscious of others, while in Hegel's recognition others-consciousness is a pre-condition for us to be able to be self-conscious. This line of Hegel's thought is applied to the dialectical relationship between the master and the slave in his *Phenomenology of Spirit*.

The importance of the individual self-interest is emphasized for the benefit of society in Adam Smith's sympathy, while the importance of the individual is negated in favour of communal unity in Hegel's recognition. Hegel believes that individuals can truly be themselves only as parts of a political community. However, Adam Smith would say that we are truly self-conscious so that we are able to be part of political community. However, recognition and sympathy have similarity in the sense that they are moral or ethical dimensions of the human self-conscious desire. Human self-conscious desire, whether it is natural self-interest of Adam Smith or rational self-consciousness of Hegel, is not an event to be achieved at any present moment but "the uniform, constant, and uninterrupted efforts" of continuously progressing to the future until the final salvation is achieved. This dialectical movement is clearly shown in Hegel's recognition, and implicitly hidden in Adam Smith's sympathy. The reason may be that their theology of economic life is different. Hegel's God is a spirit in a constant process of realizing in the world, while Adam Smith's God is a sort of Abraham's God who presides over the world.

4.4. Adam Smith's Love and Hegel's Love

There is a difference between Adam Smith and Hegel in their understanding of love. The essence of Hegel's approach to love is a rational self-realization, while a natural self-interest is at the centre of Adam Smith's understanding of love. The important but abstract idea of love is clarified in the theological foundations of their economic thoughts. If God is love, it is natural that a different understanding of God leads to a different meaning of love. A true love is not emotional but rational for Hegel, while for Adam Smith, a true love is not rational but natural in its essence.

From the perspective of Adam Smith, we cannot love each other unless we love ourselves as love is the human desire which is motivated by self-interest inherent in human nature by the wisdom of Nature. However, Hegel would say that we cannot love each other unless we love others as our desire is to be realized in a higher ethical stage in the community only through self-negation, which is overcoming and preserving self-interest. If Adam Smith says that love is not possible without self-interest, then Hegel would say that love is not possible without self-negation.

Hegel's love is something to be achieved by the rational self-consciousness. I love you because I cannot be satisfied without you. There is no guarantee that I will be satisfied and free when I love someone who loves me because my love is dependent on others who may or may not love me. It does not matter whether I am free and content in self-interest. According to Hegel, we must know how to love others before we love ourselves because our self-consciousness is to be achieved only by self-conscious reason in recognition of others. This necessary process of actualization of self-consciousness is the main reason why Hegel is so dependent on the role of the state that is the final realization of self-consciousness. In his thoughts, a natural human cannot be free; a true freedom is only possible in mutual recognition which is to be finally achieved by the absolute reason of the state where God is to be self-realized through human self-rational consciousness; his immanent God works as the cunning of reason in the world, if a human has no self-consciousness.

For Smith, however, we naturally know how to love ourselves so that we may love others because our self-interest is to be naturally given in sympathy. This natural self-interest is in his case the main reason why Adam Smith is so independent from the intervention of the state so as not to interrupt the given nature of self-interest. In his thoughts, a natural human is free and is not dependent on reason to be free; this freedom is confirmed again in mutual sympathy based on natural self-interest which is given by the Wisdom of Nature, an evidence of the goodness of God, the Creator; his transcendent God works as an invisible hand over the world. If humans have no self-interest; then, it is nothing but self-negligence rather than others-interest. Humans need to be themselves before they negate themselves and become social.

4.5. Adam Smith's Synthesis and Hegel's Dialectics

Dialectics is one of the logical methods used to approach the truth of reality. By synthesising two opposing aspects of the same reality without refuting either side of its aspects, dialectics finds a way to resolve the contradiction. If synthesis without neglecting either side of two contradicting aspects is the essence of dialectics, then we may say that both Adam Smith and Hegel are dialectical thinkers. In this section, it will be shown that Adam Smith's synthesis is less dialectical compared to that of Hegel, and that the main reason is in the differences in their theology of economics.

A Dialectical Aspect of Adam Smith's Synthesis

Adam Smith explains the complexity of the daily lives of ordinary people by referring consistently to the seemingly simple desire of self-interest. By doing this, however, he does not neglect or simplify but synthesizes the tension between vice and virtue, individuals and community, and self-love and others-love. He holds conflicting ideas together and discovers solutions by synthesizing them without leaving them in dichotomy or negating either one.

Before we discuss his synthetic approach, it is necessary to briefly rearrange his arguments to see the inner hidden structure of seemingly inconsistent explanations in his analysis of human nature. Desire of trade is an instinct for humans to be born with, and commerce is a bond of friendship for humans to better their condition, which leads to social wealth without individual intention. This simple and optimistic harmony is not the whole picture of his analysis of the nature of ordinary people. The irrationality of human desire in delusions of self-love is also discussed. However, in his thought, the tension caused by the dark side of narrow self-consciousness of human nature is not an insurmountable stumbling block. His originality is in his psychological analysis of self as a way of solution of this contradiction. The human within as the impartial spectator is introduced.[14] In mentioning this, the introduction of the impartial spectator is still far from the final solution.[15] As human reason is feeble, a higher tribunal above human reason and conscience is necessary: all-seeing God as the ultimate efficient cause. Then the essence of human nature is, for him, not just the matter of rationality or morality but a matter of religious faith.

In addition to this tension in his psychologically multi-dimensional structure of human nature, there is another inconsistency in his arguments. He emphasizes the role of vanity for economic development saying it is vanity, not ease, which interests us,[16] while he also says that it is not vanity but ease and tranquillity that are the ultimate desires of humans for the true happiness in the world to come.[17] However, this inconsistency can be understood if his hidden theology is taken into consideration.

Self-interest is the centre of this whole process of finding a solution for the tension between virtues and vices. Even the sense of propriety too

14 TMS III.3.4, III.i.6.

15 TMS III.4.6, III.4.7.

16 TMS I.iii.2.1.

17 WN II.iv.16–17, TMS VII. ii.2.11.

is well supported by the strongest motives of self-interest. In Adam Smith's thoughts, self-interest is the natural human desire of self-preservation, which is relational and harmonious for the purpose of private happiness and public welfare under the guidance of the invisible hand.[18] However, it is not monotonous, simple harmony without tension; rather, it is self-consciousness with inner tension between self-love and others-love, vanity and tranquillity, virtues and vices, faith and reason, immanence and transcendence, deception and providence, good and evil, human weakness and God's providence, this world and the world to come, etc. By utilizing the tension in human reality, he observes the human weakness of ordinary people without turning a blind eye to a telic future coming from the faith and hope in God.[19]

In addition, his approach to humans and society is realistic as he constantly refers back to experiential facts rather than to abstract theorization. However, his dependence on experience and reality is not Humean experientialism but a telic realism with faith in God's providence in the world through the strongest human instinct of self-interest, without denying God's transcendence over the world as a benevolent invisible hand.[20] Through his economic, moral, and theological approach to human behaviour, he rejects the traditional dichotomy of vice and virtue, and synthesizes from his vantage point of self-interest without truncating the tension.

Adam Smith may be unconditionally optimistic for the goodness of God; however, he also emphasizes the existence and telic role of evil and God's theodicy.[21] He may be optimistic for the future of society; however, he also says that 'it was not the wisdom and policy but the disorder and injustice of the European governments which peopled and cultivated America.'[22] He seems to be pessimistic about the role of feeble reason as a way of salvation; however, he notices the important role of the impartial spectator of conscience as a counteracting mechanism against the delusion

18 TMS II.i.5.10.
19 TMS III.ii.33.
20 WN IV.ii.9, TMS IV.i.10.
21 TMS III.3.4.
22 WN, p. IV.vii.b.61.

of self-love.[23] He believes that natural self-interest is the strongest motive of desires inherent in ordinary people by the providence of the goodness of God; however, he does not forget the weakness of human self-deception. He does not fall into the simplification of reality by self-interest as in egoism, nor does he neglect the important role of self-interest in reality as in simple altruism.

Our daily lives are not always harmonious even though we constantly desire for ease and tranquillity. We are constantly struggling with conflict in reality: body and soul, vices and virtues, reason and faith, etc. Adam Smith does not neglect the human destiny in this world; he has faith and hope in the world to come.[24] Self-interest is not simplification of the struggling reality but synthesis of the tension moving progressively for the world to come.

In sum, Adam Smith's self-interest is surely not dualistic but synthetic and almost dialectical, paying attention to the difference between feeble reason and unstable passions, and without leaving the tension between virtue and vices as antinomy. He believes that human weakness works for the happiness of the whole in his theology of economic life. Human nature and God's providence are interrelated through self-interest by an invisible hand in God's teleological plan. His idea of self-interest is neither negation of human weakness nor acquisition of human perfection; rather, it is human weakness in God's providence. Self-interest is his awareness of human weakness and his faith in God's providence.

Comparison with Hegel's Dialectics

As discussed in the previous section, Adam Smith's sympathy is a synthesis of self-interest. From Adam Smith's perspective, Hegel's self-consciousness is certainly dialectical as it is in the process of recognizing its own identity in its self-negation, so the dialectical way of thinking is pervaded in Hegel's

23 TMS III.3.21.
24 TMS III.ii.33.

thought. From Hegel's perspective, Adam Smith's self-interest is also in a sense dialectical as it constantly emphasizes the difference between humans and God, saying that humans are weak, and God is all-powerful and always good. The outcome of the conflict does not lead to the refusal of either God's goodness or human weakness, but to a synthesis or combination of the opposing assertions. In this section, it will be shown that Adam Smith's synthesis is based on the theological belief that nature is good, compared to Hegel's dialectics that is based on his theology of economic life that reason (*vernunft*) is good, and nature is evil. This theological difference will be suggested as the reason why Hegel's logic is more dialectical than Adam Smith's logic.

God's never failing goodness as Adam Smith's self-interest is a theological solution of the unmitigated tension between God above the world and humans on the earth in his theology of economic life. However, Adam Smith's self-interest is less dialectical compared to Hegel's self consciousness as it is naturally given rather than rationally realized. Self-interest and self-denial are two faces of the human self-conscious desire for salvation. Adam Smith approaches human self-consciousness from self-interest without neglecting self-denial, the other side of human consciousness, in his theology of economic life. He believes that human nature is good. Hegel however begins from self-denial without erasing the human self-conscious desire for salvation in his theology of economic life. He believes that human nature is not good.

Self-interest is a very appealing concept or language to describe the various human behaviours, not only in economics but also in many other areas. The concept of self-interest gives us a powerful tool with which we may explain all human behaviour, especially in this economic world in which economic profit is generally regarded as the only economic prophet who saves the world from the evil of the present scarcity. However, self-interest is not one-dimensional blind selfishness at all; rather self-interest as a natural instinct has moral and theological dimensions in it, as discussed in the previous chapter by analyzing the concept of Adam Smith's self-interest. Just as we can say that a human has distinct, but not separate body and soul, we can also believe that human desire has two faces of self-interest and self-denial, like a coin. For conveying the dual aspects of human behaviour, self-consciousness is a convenient concept since it describes human behaviour without neglecting the tension imbedded in human desires which have two seemingly different dimensions: self-interest and self-denial.

Hegel's self-denial is composed of three stages. The first stage is a moment that we are naturally conscious of ourselves. This stage is the same as Adam Smith's self-interest. In Hegel's thought, we are conscious of ourselves naturally; this natural self-consciousness is not sufficient as it is natural. When we are conscious of our insufficiency, we are in need of being conscious of others. This others-consciousness is meaningless unless others are conscious of themselves; and others-consciousness is inefficient unless others are conscious of us. This mutual self-consciousness is called recognition in Hegel's language. We need to recognize them so that they can recognize themselves, and in turn we are recognized by them. Then our self-consciousness is *to be realized* by *recognition*. We cannot be ourselves without mutual-recognition. According to Hegel's self-consciousness, I am conscious of you; otherwise, my self-consciousness is not to be realized. I cannot be myself without you. I recognize you because I want to be recognized by you. Recognition is a rational relationship by the development of self-consciousness. Hegel's self-consciousness and recognition is completely resonant with his understanding of God who is immanent in the world where God is to be self-realized through the rational self-consciousness of individuals.

Adam Smith's idea of self-interest is not divided as in Hegel. We are naturally aware of us. This self-interest is necessary and sufficient in itself as it is natural. We are conscious of others not because we feel insufficient in our self-consciousness but because we are conscious of ourselves. We cannot be conscious of others unless we are conscious of ourselves, and we do not need others' recognition of us or our recognition of others for us to be conscious of ourselves. We can be ourselves by ourselves. Then our self-consciousness is *to be given* by *nature*. We can be conscious of others because we are conscious of ourselves. The relationship with others is called sympathy in Adam Smith's language. According to Adam Smith's self-interest, I have interest in you because I have interest in myself. I have sympathy because I have self-interest. Sympathy is a natural relationship by the development of self-interest. Adam Smith's self-interest and sympathy is again perfectly congruent to his understanding of God. His God is transcendent over the world. The never-failing goodness of God works through the natural self-interest of individuals. In this sense, we may say that economics, morality, and theology are interrelated in Adam Smith's thought. The reading of Adam Smith's works by mainstream economics is however heavily influenced by economic rationality to the point that the moral and theological concepts are simplified and erased out of human desire for the beauty of theoretical simplicity. We may have sympathy for the arduous effort to make economic theory persuasive and efficient when we consider that the conflicting concepts such as God's transcendence and immanence are hard to manipulate in economics and even in theology as well.

Adam Smith is concerned with the principles related to the experiential facts in our daily lives while Hegel's concern is about the reality beneath the existing appearance. When Adam Smith introduces the concept of self-interest to convey his ideas about human behaviour in society, he begins from the natural facts that people experience in their daily lives. It is natural for him to begin his approach from the front face of the human desire, self-interest, without denying the moral and theological dimension of it. This prudential aspect of Adam Smith's self-interest is the point Fleischacker (1999) pertinently points out in his book.[25] Even though he does not mention the theological dimension of self-interest in explaining how self-interest guides us towards certain cognitive abilities, the essence of Adam Smith's self-interest is the freedom of judgement.[26] Hegel, however, approaches from the other side of the human behaviour. It is rational for him to analyze from the other side of the human desire. If Adam Smith says that men cannot be themselves without self-interest, Hegel would say that men cannot be themselves without self-denial.

If Hegel talks about God's justice and community, then Adam Smith would mention God's grace and individuals. If Adam Smith talks about the affluence of the commercial market, then Hegel would talk about poverty

25 Samuel Fleischacker, *A Third Concept of Liberty: Judgment and Freedom in Kant and Adam Smith* (Princeton, NJ: Princeton University Press, 1999), 135.

26 Ibid., 7–8.

as its result. If Hegel brings up rational self-consciousness as virtue to be accomplished, then Adam Smith would mention natural self-interest as a given instinct. If Hegel criticises self-interest as evil selfishness, then Adam Smith would say that self-interest is related to the goodness of God. If Hegel talks about reason as virtue, then Adam Smith would mention the weakness of reason. If Hegel says that the pivotal concept corresponding to the reality of human desire is self-consciousness, then Adam Smith would say that the focal concept corresponding to the reality of human desire is self-interest. If Hegel comes up with the verse, 'Get these out of here! How dare you turn my Father's house into a market!' (John 2:16), then Adam Smith would quote from the verse 'Why then didn't you put my money on deposit, so that when I came back, I could have collected it with interest?' (Luke 19:23)

To sum up, Hegel's dialectics is clearly shown in his theology of economic life. The original state of humans and God's providence contradict each other as the former is natural and the latter is rational (*vernunftig*). Self-conscious desire is to be both negated and preserved in a dialectical process of rational self-consciousness in the civil society and finally in the state in Hegel's theology of economic life. The natural state of humans is not completely negated but somehow in harmony with the Wisdom of Reason (*vernunft*). That is God's providence that works through self-consciousness. This is called cunning of reason (*vernunft*) in his theology of economic life. Adam Smith's dialectics is implicitly shown in his theology of economic life. The original state of humans and God's providence is in harmony as the former is embedded in human nature by the Wisdom of Nature. The human self-conscious desire is however not human rational ability but natural weakness in Adam Smith's theology of economics. Therefore, the human weakness is preserved and overcome in harmony with the Wisdom of Nature. This is beyond human ability, but it works through self-interest in God's providence. This is referred to as the invisible hand in his theology of economic life.

4.6. Summary and Conclusion

The similar but different approaches of two main thinkers' to human self-conscious desire in relation to salvation give us some clues to explore the meaningful dialogue between economics and theology. No matter whether it be the commercial market or the communal society, our life is not solipsistic but relational. When we turn to the relationship between individuals, sympathy and recognition (*Anerkennung*) have been notified respectively in Adam Smith and Hegel's theology of economics.

The essence of human relationships is natural sympathy for Adam Smith and rational (*vernunftig*) recognition for Hegel. Sympathy is a moral emotion embedded in human nature by the providence of God in Adam Smith's theology of economic life, while recognition (*Anerkennung*) is an ethical reason (*vernunft*) to be realized in the development of human self-consciousness in the community. Love is an emotion based on sympathy in Adam Smith's thought and recognition in Hegel's. The self-conscious desire is the main motive flowing through the moral or ethical dimension of human relationships in both Adam Smith and Hegel's thoughts. However, sympathy is fundamentally natural in Adam Smith's thought, and recognition is rational (*vernunftig*) in Hegel's. The dialectical structure of the human relationship is the result of the two faces of human self-conscious desire. Therefore, it is weak and implicit for Adam Smith, but strong and explicit in Hegel. This bifurcation is caused by the differences of their theological precepts.

Hegel's recognition is a dialectical process as it is dependent on self-negation, while Adam Smith's sympathy is less dialectical as it is based on natural self-interest. Hegel's uniqueness in his understanding of human desire is in his effort to harmonize the seemingly conflicting human desires between self-interest and communal interest. By doing so, Hegel achieves his own ethical system based on self-interest. Self-interest is necessary, but to be overcome in the ethical life through corporations in the civil society and then through the state. Self-interest is introduced as a necessary step for preparing a way for higher institutions such as the corporations and the state. This is the difference between Hegel's approach to self-interest and Adam Smith's.

Adam Smith believes that self-interest stands alone without human virtue coming from rational reason, while Hegel believes that self-interest is not only to be preserved but also to be overcome by the development of rational self-consciousness. In spite of the economic and moral dimensions of self-interest commonly shared by Hegel and Adam Smith, Hegel's self-interest is different from Adam Smith's. Hegel believes that self-interest is both to be preserved and overcome through institutions such as the corporation and the state, while Adam Smith argues that self-interest is to be preserved rather than overcome by any exterior institutions. Hegel notices the potency of the economic dimension of Adam Smith's self-interest, and mistakenly believes that his ethical approach to self-interest is better than Adam Smith's explanation which is, according to Hegel, just an approximation of the reality of human behaviour. Hegel's self-consciousness is human desire to be developed by rational reason in providential self-actualization of God in the world, while Adam Smith's self-interest is human desire to be given as an instinct by the providential wisdom of God over the world.

In conclusion, it is certainly true that we experience tension between self-interest and self-negation in everyday life. Adam Smith's sympathy and Hegel's recognition give us an idea about how the conflict between individual benefit and social welfare is solved in the human relationship based on the human self-conscious desire. However, the different explanations of the structure of the moral relationship based on the same human self-conscious desire illuminates the reality of human existence in the world. Adam Smith's sympathy and Hegel's recognition show that the economic, moral, and theological relationship is based on the human self-conscious desire. Economics and Theology need to be interrelated to understand the human behaviour not only in the market but also in the moral and religious world.

CHAPTER 5

Invisible Hand and Cunning of Reason: God's Providence

There have been many scholarly debates about Adam Smith's invisible hand and Hegel's cunning of reason. Both of them are generally regarded as strange and awkward expressions seemingly unfamiliar with their own systems of thought. The aim of this chapter is to clarify the problematic but important concepts from the perspective of the theology of economic life in Adam Smith and Hegel. What do Adam Smith and Hegel actually mean by the invisible hand and the cunning of reason respectively? How do they use these expressions in their theology of economic life? Is there any similarity or difference between these two mystical and problematic terms? This chapter is an answer to those questions.

Other works of research have compared and analyzed the possible similarities and differences between Adam Smith's invisible hand and Hegel's cunning of reason, for example, Hollis (1987), Davis (1989), and Ullmann-Margalit (1997). This relatively unexplored area is however worth careful attention as it may clarify the relationship between economics and theology, and help to understand the meaning of salvation from the perspective of the theology of economic life. In this chapter, a different approach is taken, for the theological aspect of the human self-conscious desire is missing or neglected in those previous research works in spite of their contribution to this issue. Self-interest and salvation are used as two main conceptual tools to decode the meaning hidden in Adam Smith's invisible hand and Hegel's cunning of reason.

Three main arguments suggested in this chapter are as follows: firstly, Adam Smith's invisible hand is the providence of the transcendent God, while Hegel's cunning of reason is the providence of the immanent God. Secondly, Adam Smith's invisible hand and Hegel's cunning of reason are neither ironic nor contradictory, but at the centre of the theological foundations of their economic thoughts. Thirdly, Adam Smith's invisible hand and Hegel's cunning of reason cannot be properly understood without taking into account the theological aspect of the human self-conscious desire. This chapter will conclude that God's providence and the human self-conscious desire are neither bifurcated nor neglected but interrelated and united through the invisible hand and the cunning of reason respectively in their theologies of economic life. The cunning of reason is Hegel's expression showing the theological aspect of his thought about the role of the human passions that are in harmony with social welfare. It implies that human passions contribute to the development of the historical process. The invisible hand, however, is Adam Smith's term that is introduced to explain expected social benefit in spite of the self-interested behaviour of individuals.

5.1. Invisible Hand as the Providence of the Transcendent God

In chapters 2 and 4, it is shown that human nature and God's providence are the two main poles supporting Adam Smith's idea that self-interest is a way of salvation. In addition, it is emphasized that self-interest is a theological relationship with God in Adam Smith's theology of economics. Now, we are ready to discuss the role of invisible hand. What is the meaning of invisible hand in Adam Smith's works? How does he use the concept of the invisible hand to convey his important economic and theological ideas? Is it possible for us to recognize any consistency of the invisible hand in his works? These are the main questions to be discussed in this section. Adam Smith is the pioneer opening up the new horizon of modern economics in which the rational choice theory is hailed as the best tool we have for maximizing not only individual satisfaction but also social benefit. We all live in the economized society. A theological dimension of human economic life is not the main issue in the market any more. The pursuit of self-interest to maximize one's own utility is the best and final norm for an economic human. Being baptized by the economic rationality, it is not easy for us to hear the music or see the world that Adam Smith tries to show and play with the invisible hand that surely has a theological flavour of his time. What kinds of meaning does he try to convey with the idea of the invisible hand? Can we see the world hidden in his theology of economics under a theological umbrella of the invisible hand? Or, is it nothing but an ironic joke? It will be argued that the invisible hand is the theological link connecting human self-interest with God's providence in his theology of economics.

Self-interest and the Invisible Hand

There has been considerable scholarly debate regarding the nature of the invisible hand in Adam Smith's works. Davis (1989) points out that the invisible hand makes the theological premise explicit. However, it is a hiding place defying rational investigation (Davis 1989), an ironic theological connotation (Ullmann-Margalit 1997), and an ironic joke throughout all three cases (Rothschild 1994, 2001), an inducement for a merchant to keep capital at home (Gramp 2000). These arguments do not take into account the theological aspect of Adam Smith's thought. There are however other arguments emphasizing the theological nature in Adam Smith's works; for example, Kleer (2000) and Hill (2001, 2004). Hill tries to show that there is a hidden theology in Adam Smith's works especially in relation to theodicy, a problem of evil. If so, we may say that Adam Smith is probably a natural theologian (Long, 2006).

I basically agree with the argument that the teleological nature is embedded in Adam Smith's thought. In this section, however, more attention is to be paid to the theological dimension of human self-conscious desire as a way of salvation in Adam Smith's theology of economic life. Invisible hand cannot be properly understood without taking into account the theological dimension of self-interest discussed in chapter 2. By illuminating the hidden theology embedded in Adam Smith's invisible hand from a vantage point of salvation, we may see the world he has in his mind and listen to the music he tries to play with the flute of invisible hand. It will be argued that Adam Smith's invisible hand is the providence of the transcendent God in his theology of economic life. In other words, the invisible hand is not ornamental or ironic, but it is his theological precept on which his economic ideas are built on.

The relationship between self-interest and God's providence has not been paid the attention it deserves so far in spite of its importance in understanding Adam Smith's thought in general and the invisible hand in particular. One of the reasons may be in our hesitation to enter the unfamiliar interdisciplinary area. Even though Adam Smith's self-interest is generally assumed as an economic rationality in modern economics, some catch from it an emotional or moral aspect such as a warm sentiment. Rothschild argues that Adam Smith himself did not pay particular attention to the invisible hand, and that the image of the invisible hand is best interpreted as a mildly ironic joke.[1] The relationship between self-interest and God's providence in Adam Smith's thought is broken in her analysis of self-interest as a warm sentiment and the invisible hand as an ironic joke.

Vivenza's argument is another good example showing the difficulty of relating self-interest with God's providence in Adam Smith's thought.[2] She approaches Adam Smith's ideas in relation to classical backgrounds including not just Stoic but also Epicurean and Aristotelian thought. According to her argument, Adam Smith is closer to Stoicism than to the Epicureanism as long as God's providence is concerned, because Adam Smith is convinced of providence in nature. However, she continues to argue that Adam Smith is in line with Epicureanism rather than Stoicism as far as human nature is concerned, because he believes that the main motive of human behaviour is natural feeling not rational reason. Natural self-interest and God's providence is bifurcated again in her approach to Adam Smith's thought.

1 Emma Rothschild, *Economic Sentiments: Adam Smith, Condorcet and the Enlightenment* (Harvard, MA: Harvard University Press, 2001).

2 Gloria Vivenza, *Adam Smith and the Classics: The Classical Heritage in Adams Smith's Thought* (Oxford: Oxford University Press, 2001).

On the surface, Adam Smith's theological foundations of his economic thoughts seem to be close to natural religion rather than to the personal God of revelation. If so, his ethics and theology seem to be predominantly Stoic or Epicurean rather than Christian. The human self-conscious desire and God's providence is disconnected.

This bifurcation between self-interest and God's providence becomes clear as she argues that Adam Smith's position in religion is ambiguous as he says little about theology itself in his works, although all that he says is orthodox. Her argument is based on her belief that the self-autonomy of Stoicism contrasts with Christianity's dependence on the grace of God, as Christians cannot act on their own, compared to the Stoics who do not recognize any external authority. She then naturally concludes that Adam Smith's self-interest is not Stoic reason, Aristotelian mediocrity, nor Christian obedience, but Epicurean pleasure. The relationship between self-interest and God's providence is broken in her analysis of self-interest as a natural feeling and the invisible hand as providence. This is the merit of Vivenza's approach, which shows the providential aspect of Adam Smith's thought in relation to Stoicism and Epicureanism. However, her approach depends on her own belief that Christians cannot act on their own. According to her belief, self-autonomy is the name of Epicurean, Aristotelian or Stoic thought, but not of Christian thought, because, she believes, Christianity depends on the grace of God. Here we are able to feel again the never-ending tension between self-autonomy and telos, self-interest and self-denial, human achievement and God's gift.

In a sense, it may be true that humans are dependent on God for our salvation by definition. However, it does not necessarily mean that self-interest is against God's grace. Adam Smith argues that God's wisdom is above our rational ability.[3] Invisible hand is a theological link connecting human self-conscious desire with God's providence over the world in his thought. In Adam Smith's theology of economics, self-interest is not just a single-minded profit maximization without any direction, but it is teleological in the sense that it is embedded in human nature by God's provi-

3 TMS II.ii.3.5.

dence. Adam Smith's self-interest is a way of salvation for individuals and society, because it is teleological rather than a blind profit-maximization without future. It has a teleological dimension, because self-interest is a gift from God who is always all-knowing, all powerful, and always good in his thought. In Adam Smith's world view, this world is created by God who has a purpose for human happiness. He believes that self-interest is human nature given by God's providence. For Adam Smith, self-interest is not something to be acquired by human wisdom or reason; rather, it is a gift from the Creator who has telos of human salvation.

Adam Smith's self-interest may have a face of self-autonomy as it is natural feeling, warm sentiment, or even economic rationality. The point is however not in its face but its content. Adam Smith's God is the Creator whose goodness never fails regardless of whether they are kings or beggars. This theme is constantly repeated in his works. Self-interest is a way of salvation in his theology of economic life, not because it is self-autonomy or the rational ability of humans but because it is, he strongly believes, the gift from God, the Wisdom of Nature, who knows human weakness and never leaves them without care and love. Self-interest is the gift from God in Adam Smith's theology of economic life. In addition, his God is transcendent. Self-interest is the gift of the transcendent God whose goodness never fails in presiding over the world through the invisible hand. Consequently, there is a connection between self-interest and God's providence. The invisible hand is not ornamental. It is in essence his theological link connecting self-interest with God's providence. Invisible hand is the providence of the transcendent God, and self-interest is God's teleological gift for human weakness in his theology of economic life.

Invisible Hand as the Providence of the Transcendent God

Self-interest and salvation are again the main conceptual tools with which to decode the role and meaning of the invisible hand in relation to God's providence and human nature, the two main poles for the human self-conscious desire in Adam Smith's theology of economic life. The self-conscious desire is embedded in human nature by God's providence for human salvation.

Self-interest is the gift of God whose goodness never fails in his theology of economic life. The invisible hand is the providence of the transcendent God in Adam Smith's theology of economic life. The invisible hand is not an ironic joke but the essence of Adam Smith's theology of economic life. It is his conceptual tool conveying his theological belief that there is always a solution and way for salvation in spite of the conflict and tension between the never-failing goodness of God's providence and the weakness of human nature. Without his belief in invisible hand, it is not possible for him to argue confidently and consistently that self-interest is a way of salvation for individuals and society.

For Adam Smith, the invisibility of a transcendent God in our daily experiences means neither that there is no divine providence in the world, nor that God is such a person to be manipulated by human reason. We are not forsaken without the Wisdom of God in spite of the seeming contingency and arbitrariness in the world. Here, self-interest is given as a contact point between God's providence and human weakness. For Adam Smith, self-interest is a gift given to human weakness. God is invisible and beyond manipulation but with a hand of providence as the Creator. In this sense, Adam Smith's invisible hand is not a joke, but the divine providence of the Creator. The invisible hand cannot be properly understood without the theological dimension of self-interest. Self-interest is at the centre of his theological foundations of economic thought.

It is because of our own reading into his richly unified apprehension of the world of the daily lives of the ordinary people of his time without taking into account his theological foundations that his economic, moral and theological dimensions seem to be mutually contradictory. For him, self-interest is the common motive in the daily lives of the ordinary people whether it is economic, moral, or religious. The invisible hand is not in conflict with other parts of his works; rather, it is a theological belief permeated throughout all his works. The invisible hand is neither capricious nor just a order-preserving force, but it is the providence of the transcendent God the Creator by whom humans are created in the image of God and is given the consciousness of self-interest as a way of salvation. Without this theological perspective, Adam Smith's works cannot stand as a whole, nor can we understand the reason why both faith and joy are frequently discovered in his explanation of the seemingly contradictory reality of the daily lives of many ordinary people in his works. From the rational perspective of our own time heavily baptised by the one-dimensional economic rationality, the invisible hand may be unnecessary, annoying, or an ironic joke; however, it is for him the providential hand of God as the Wisdom of Nature whether our rational reason knows it or not.

To sum up, the role of the concept of invisible hand in Adam Smith's works cannot be recognized unless we take into account the theological dimension of the human self-conscious desire in his theology of economic life. Self-interest is not just economic rationality, but it is also moral sympathy and theological faith. Self-interest is a way of salvation in his theology of economics. The original state of humans is in harmony with God's providence as self-interest is innate instinct in human nature by the Wisdom of Nature. The human self-conscious desire is however not human rational ability but natural weakness in Adam Smith's theology of economics. Therefore, the human weakness is to be somehow preserved and overcome without negating self-interest to be in harmony with the Wisdom of Nature. This is beyond human ability but in God's providence that works through natural self-interest. This is called the invisible hand in his thought. The invisible hand is the providence of the transcendent God in his theology of economic life.

5.2. Consistency of the Invisible Hand in Adam Smith's Works

Interestingly, Adam Smith's three cases of the invisible hand are from three different contexts: an economic context in *The Wealth of Nations*, a moral context in *The Theory of Moral Sentiments*, and a theological one from *Essays on Philosophical Subjects*. It is generally argued that there is no unified notion or consistency in Adam Smith's three explicit references to the individual hand (Macfie 1971; Gramp 2000; Rothschild 2001). However, the seeming inconsistency is not because of Adam Smith's problem in handling the concept of the invisible hand; rather, it might be because of our own economic reading of his ideas from our own rational perspectives without consideration of his theological aspect of self-interest. Let us see whether there is a unity among the three cases. The three aspects of Adam Smith's self-interest are discussed in the previous chapter. Interestingly, we may note that the three cases of the invisible hand in his works correspond to economic, moral, and theological aspects respectively.

The Invisible Hand and the Economic Aspect of God's Providence

The first case of the invisible hand comes from his work *The Wealth of Nations*. The expression 'invisible hand' is mentioned just once in his whole book that discusses many economic issues from the perspective of individual self-interest. Even though it is a rarely used expression in the book, he introduces it in the economic context of capital flow between domestic and overseas. It is related to the natural emotion of individuals who prefer the support of the domestic to that of foreign industry.[4] Self-interest is related to the invisible hand.

Importantly, the use of the invisible hand is closely related to the human self-conscious desire. The invisible hand in this passage is not an awkward intervention of God, but the natural providence of the transcendent God whose goodness never fails for human salvation, for he argues that our pursuing of own interest is led by the invisible hand to promote public welfare more effectually than we really intend to promote it. In Adam Smith's theology of economic life, self-interest is an inherent desire given by the wisdom of God whose goodness never fails. Self-interest is God's gift. God's providential gift is shown in human self-conscious desire by the invisible hand in his theology of economic life. The role of the invisible hand in his works is easily misunderstood or overlooked unless the theological aspect of self-interest is taken into consideration. Self-interest is the gift from the grace of God whose goodness is hidden in the invisible hand but never fails for our salvation in this world or in a world to come

4 WN IV.ii.9.

in his theology of economics. Of course, it is our choice whether we see his world from our own one-dimensional horizon of economic rationality without consideration of any moral and theological aspect. However, we may see an unexpected world in his theology of economic life, in which economics and theology are not bifurcated but united as one. This theology of economic life may give us a better understanding of what salvation is. The invisible hand is the providence of the transcendent God who works through the human self-conscious desire that is thoroughly permeated throughout his theology of economic life.

God's goodness is permeated in his self-interest in his theology of economic life. His self-interest, therefore, is the beginning and end of the market. Caring for social welfare is the unintended result of human self-conscious desire. Therefore, the invisibility of God's providence is natural for Adam Smith's theology of economics. However, Hegel's approach to human self-conscious desire is very much dyed with his own idea of God's self-realization in the world. The self-conscious desire may be the beginning of the market, but surely not the end in his civil society.

The Invisible Hand and the Moral Aspect of God's Providence

The second case of the individual hand comes from his book *The Theory of Moral Sentiments* that deals with his moral philosophy. The exact expression 'invisible hand' is rarely used in the book. There is just one case in which it is mentioned. In that particular case, an invisible hand is introduced to explain the distribution of wealth.[5] It emphasizes the role of self-interest for the interest of the society without intending it. Thus, it is possible to recognize again in his argument of this specific context that the invisible hand is related to the role of self-interest for salvation. In this case, the providential nature of the invisible hand is shown more clearly than in the previous work as he says that God's providence neither forgets nor abandons the poor in his distribution. God's goodness is emphasized again in his never-failing concern for human salvation in his theology of economic life. More importantly, such graceful care is not the result of human rational

5 TMS IV.I.10.

ability but the unexpected consequence of the human self-conscious desire. In his theological world, our self-interest for vain and insatiable desires is led by the invisible hand to share the same happiness of human life among the rich, the poor, the kings, and the beggars without intending it. God's providence is the essence of the invisible hand, which works through the natural desire for self-interest rather than rational ability in his theology of economic life. Consequently, we may conclude that the invisible hand in this passage is exactly consistent with the one in the previous passage in the sense that the invisible hand is God's providence working through self-interest in his theology of economic life.

Adam Smith's morality in his *The Theory of Moral Sentiments* is different from Hegel's ethical life (*Sittlichkeit*) in his *Philosophy of Right*, for the former is related to sympathy which is based on self-interest, and the latter is related to mutual recognition based on self-consciousness. However, both of these concepts have their origins in God's providence: the former from the natural providence of the Wisdom of Nature, the latter from the rational (*vernunftig*) providence of the Wisdom of Reason (*vernunft*). Adam Smith's invisible hand is the providence of the transcendent God, while Hegel's cunning of reason is the providence of the immanent God. We cannot see the consistency of invisible hand in the three main works unless the theological dimension of self-interest is taken into account. Three cases of the invisible hand has constituency in his theology of economics.

The Invisible Hand and the Religious Aspect of God's Providence

The third but chronologically first reference to the invisible hand in Adam Smith's writings comes from his *Essays on Philosophical Subjects*, a collection of his unpublished works. The *History of Astronomy* is the largest one of the three works contained in it. As he explains the origin of philosophy in the book, the invisible hand is used in the religious or theological context in which the Polytheistic religions attribute only irregular events such as lightening and storms to the invisible hand of their gods.[6]

6 EPS III.2.

The idea of the invisible hand of Jupiter has a religious or theological flavour, but certainly has no relation to the individual hand working in the market as in the *The Wealth of Nations* and *The Theory of Moral Sentiments.* In this case, there is seemingly no direct relation between self-interest and the invisible hand compared to the previous cases. Then the question is: is the seemingly theological concept of the invisible hand just an irony without any consistency in his works? How can we use the conceptual tools of self-interest and salvation to decode the hidden meaning of the invisible hand embedded in Adam Smith's works to explain its role consistently in his theology of economics?

To see the consistency of invisible hand in his works, we need to pay attention to the theological dimension of self-interest in his theology of economic life, which is discussed in chapter 2. Human self-conscious desire is still at the centre of the seemingly inconsistent introduction of the invisible hand of Jupiter. It is implied in his passage quoted above that the savages have self-conscious desire as they ascribe the more irregular events of nature such as thunder and lightning, for example, to the favour or displeasure of their gods. In his invisible hand of Jupiter, we may see the locus of self-conscious desire embedded in the religious behaviour of the savages who ascribe the irregular events to their gods. They become more self-conscious in experiencing the irregular events such as lightning and thunder rather than in regular phenomena. This line of thought is more developed as he says that philosophy helps humans to expand the self-conscious desire to the area of the regular events.[7] The self-conscious desire is the main motive of both the religious behaviour of the savages and the pursuit of philosophy. The invisible hand used with Jupiter is again consistently related to the human self-conscious desire in his theology of economic life. The meaning and role of the invisible hand in his works is not to be properly understood or decoded without its relation to the theological dimension of the human self-conscious desire.

7 EPS III.3.

5.3. Cunning of Reason as the Providence of the Self-realizing God

In the chapters 3 and 4, it is shown that human reason and God's providence are the two main poles of his idea that self-consciousness is a way of salvation. We are now ready to deal with the seemingly problematic concept: the cunning of reason. What is the role of cunning of reason in his thought? Why does he use this seemingly strange idea, which seems to be difficult to fit into his system of thought that is based on the strong faith in the power of reason (*vernunft*)? This is the question of this section.

The cunning of reason is Hegel's way of dealing with God's providential intervention into the world which is in the process of development by rational (*vernunftig*) self-consciousness in his theology of economic life. It is his conceptual tool with which to convey his theological belief that there is always a solution and way for salvation in spite of the conflict between human nature as evil and human reason as good. Without the cunning of reason, it is probably not possible for him to argue that self-consciousness is a way of salvation for individuals and society. The cunning of reason is his theological precept with which to deal with God's wisdom hidden in the human economic life that is in constant movement but always in God's providence.

Hegel's God is immanent in the rational (*vernunftig*) world of the state; however, the role of human passions such as self-interest is not something to be useless in the development of human history but useful as an instrument in God's providence. Self-interest as human passion, then, is a sort of cunning in Hegel's idea of a rational (*vernunftig*) God. Adam Smith's God is transcendent and invisible in the natural world; however, we are left with self-interest which is the providential guidance inherent in our nature by the wisdom of God: God's helping hand.

'The stone the builders rejected has become the capstone; the Lord has done this, and it is marvellous in our eyes' (Mark 12:10–11). This is a part of speech in the parable given to the people who question the valid authority of Jesus' mission. It is true that we sometimes do not know what we are doing. In spite of our ignorance and selfishness, however, the world keeps going on its own track. In Hegel, there is a similar expression in his thoughts to imply this irony of human history: the cunning of reason.[8]

There are different approaches to understanding the cunning of reason in Hegel's thought. The cunning of reason seems to be one of the mystical concepts to be decoded in Hegel's ideas, for it does not seem to be resonant with his rational (*vernunftig*) self-consciousness. This seeming inconsistency in Hegel's cunning of reason is sometimes at the centre of scholarly debate. Avineri argues that Hegel's cunning of reason is an inconsistent language since there is a contradiction in Hegel's doctrine of the historical individuals of the world, who are fully conscious of the idea when he realizes it, at other times only instinctively or unconsciously.[9] However, Taylor thinks that the cunning of reason in Hegel's thoughts is far from being incomprehensible; rather, he believes that it is indispensable for any theory of history in which unconscious motivation is given a role.[10]

The cunning of reason is often compared with the invisible hand of Adam Smith, which is regarded as a problematic or unnecessary expression by many of the mainstream economists who believe that the economic theory of Adam Smith is able to be understood without such a troublesome concept related to God. John B. Davis argues that there are similarities in the invisible hand of Adam Smith and the cunning of reason of Hegel as they are used as conceptual tools to explain that the action of self interest in the economic world creates something greater than their sum, something desired yet unintended. He also points out that both Adam Smith and Hegel depend on the divine providence through the invisible hand and the cunning of reason respectively because there is no other way for uniting self-interest and social welfare, especially in case of dealing with a combination of a value-free part and a value-laden whole. In this vein, Davis concludes that the invisible hand and the cunning of reason have

8 G.W.F. Hegel, *The philosophy of history* (New York: Dover, 1956), 33.

9 Shlomo Avineri, *Hegel's Theory of the Modern State* (New York: Cambridge University Press, 1972).

10 Charles Taylor, *Hegel and Modern Society* (New York: Cambridge University Press, 1979), 100.

instability and discourage rational investigation by evading the human responsibility and depending on the divine providence for reconciling the possible conflict between private interest and general welfare.[11]

In contrast to Davis' approach that emphasizes the similarities, Ullmann-Margalit concentrates on the dissimilarities between the invisible hand and the cunning of reason.[12] She argues that these two ideas have profoundly different functions despite superficial similarity. On the surface, both ideas have the same focus on the fact that self-interest leads to general welfare by an ultimate design without any individual intention. However, she argues that there is an important difference between the invisible hand and the cunning of reason. Hegel's cunning of reason is applied to the actions of the historical heroes in the spiritual history, and explains how history uses the results of the actions of a few heroic humans to unfold the execution of God's providence, while Adam Smith's invisible hand is related to the social order, and explains how social welfare comes about as the result of the actions of numerous ordinary humans without any purpose whatsoever.

There are some interesting points in these different approaches to the relationship between the invisible hand and the cunning of reason. Although their conclusions are different in many ways, it is agreed that both the cunning of reason and the invisible hand are the conceptual tools with which to find out a solution for the tension between individual passion and social welfare, regardless of whether it is related to human history in general or social order in particular, or whether it is about a few heroes or many ordinary humans. The difference may be due to their different theology of economics. The theological foundations of political economic thoughts are at the centre of this issue.

Davis' main concern is in explaining the mechanism of how self-interest is related to divine providence through the cunning of reason and the

11 John B. Davis, 'Smith's Invisible Hand and Hegel's Cunning of Reason', *International Journal of Social Economics*, 16/6 (1989), 50–66.

12 Ullmann-Margalit, 'The Invisible Hand and the Cunning of Reason', *Social Research* 64 (Summer 1997), 182–198.

invisible hand. He uses the concept of self-interest in Hegel's *The Philosophy of Right* as a contact point to compare to the invisible hand shown in Adam Smith's three works: *The Wealth of Nations*, *The Theory of Moral Sentiments*, and *The History of Astronomy*. He then extends it to *The Philosophy of History*. His conclusion is that human responsibility is regretfully replaced by a divine providence in the works of Adam Smith and Hegel.

However, Ullmann-Margalit's main concern is in a divine providence itself; that is, the role to be explained and the domain to be applied by the invisible hand and the cunning of reason. She deals with the cunning of reason in the context of *Philosophy of History* without mentioning *Philosophy of Right*. Her conclusion is that there are important differences in their similar roles between the cunning of reason and the invisible hand. According to her conclusion, the former is about spiritual history as the result of the development of self-consciousness and the actions of a few heroic humans with God's design; the latter is about social order as the result of the actions of numerous ordinary humans without any design.

There are three important issues that are essential for us to clarify the relationship between the invisible hand and the cunning of reason: Hegel's self-consciousness and Adam Smith's self-interest, Hegel's civil society and Adam Smith's commercial market, and Hegel's God and Adam Smith's God. It does not seem to be possible to systematically compare the meanings of the invisible hand and the cunning of reason without first clarifying these essential differences between Hegel and Adam Smith in their theology of economic life.

Firstly, Hegel's self-consciousness is not the same as Adam Smith's self-interest. The former is basically something *to be achieved* by the development of human consciousness through mutual recognition in the ethical society of the state. The state is for Hegel the march of God who is to be realized in the world (PR 258 addition). Adam Smith's self-interest, however, is innate instinct *to be given* by the wisdom of Nature of God who is transcendent.

Secondly, Hegel's civil society is different from Adam Smith's commercial market. Of course, Hegel's self-consciousness also has an economic dimension in itself as in Adam Smith's self-interest, and self-interest is to be preserved in the civil society and transcended in the state in Hegel's ideas. However, the critical point worth our attention here is that self-interest is generally *preserved* in the civil society but *transcended* in the state, not as a separate stage but as a simultaneous moment in Hegel's thoughts, compared to Adam Smith whose self-interest is a universal principle as it is given by the wisdom of Nature.

Thirdly, Hegel's God is immanent to be realized in the world without which there is no God in his theology of economic life. God without the world is not real for him. His God is self-realizing Reason (*vernunft*), whose never-failing wisdom is embedded in the human self-conscious desire by God's providence. This is the cunning of reason in Hegel's theology of economic life. Compared to this, Adam Smith has faith in the transcendent God. His God is the self-sufficient Creator, whose never-failing goodness is embedded in human self-conscious desire. This is the invisible hand in Adam Smith's theology of economic life. Consequently, God's providence and the human self-conscious desire are neither bifurcated nor neglected but interrelated and united in their theology of economic life.

Hegel's understanding of human self-consciousness is based on his own theological foundations regarding humans, the world, and God. This world is the real place where God is to be realized with the development of human self-conscious desire. The economic dimension of Hegel's self-consciousness is regarded as a natural desire such as passion, impulsion, intuition, and instinct. This instinct works for itself in human history, which Hegel calls the cunning of reason in his *Philosophy of History*. This may be the reason why Taylor assumes that the cunning of reason is not incomprehensible but indispensable as he says that Hegel uses the word 'instinct' for the unconscious recognition of significance. Of course, there is no discussion about how Hegel's language of instinct might be related to Adam Smith's self-interest in Taylor's book *Hegel*. Taylor emphasizes the idea of *instinct* for the validity of the expression of the cunning of reason in Hegel's thoughts, using some examples of the historical heroes of the world. Instinct is however not a passion that belongs to the historical heroes only, but a general self-conscious desire of the many ordinary people of the civil society.

This is the point of Davis' approach to the relationship between the cunning of reason and the invisible hand. He does not limit the cunning of reason to the historical heroes but extends it to the individual self-interest of the civil society, discussing its role in Hegel's *Philosophy of Right*. By applying the cunning of reason to the human self-conscious desire, he properly points out that the cunning of reason is in essence theological as it is related to God's providence. He also compares it to the invisible hand, and shows that the invisible hand is again theological in all of three cases of Adam Smith's works as it is related to God's providence. In contrast to Davis's approach, Ullmann-Margalit's approach to the cunning of reason is not the matter of instinct of ordinary humans as in Taylor's or the human desire for self-interest in the market as in Davis', but a matter of the ever-growing self-understanding of humans; that is, rational (*vernunftig*) self-consciousness. Ullmann-Margalit therefore argues that there is a clear differentiation in their roles and domains between the cunning of reason related to a few historical heroes and the invisible hand related to ordinary people. Davis however argues that there is a similarity in that both of them have common theological backgrounds. He concludes that the unity between self-interest and social welfare is a human project, but it is wrongly replaced with a divine providence defying a rational investigation in Adam Smith's invisible hand and Hegel's cunning of reason.

However, both arguments do not seem to pay enough attention to the theological foundations of the economic thoughts in Adam Smith and Hegel. The connecting point between God's providence and the human self-conscious desire is missing. Both Hegel's self-consciousness and Adam Smith's self-interest have economic, moral, and theological dimensions. The human self-conscious desire has various colours. We may deal with them separately, but our own reading is inevitably one-sided unless we see the three different aspects together. Of course, Davis' argument points out the theological dimensions of the cunning of reason and the invisible hand. However, the theological aspect of human self-conscious desire is missing in his argument. He does not seem to give much attention to the importance of the theological precepts embedded in their analysis of the human self-conscious desire. Their theological ideas are permeated in their economic thoughts. The theological aspect of the human self-conscious desire is essential in understanding its role for salvation and its relationship with God's providence. The human self-conscious desire is a way of salvation for individuals and society in their theology of economic life.

The invisible hand or the cunning of reason is not a hiding place at all. Hegel and Adam Smith do not hide in divine providence. Rational investigation is not ignored. They believe that a human project of harmonizing between self-interest and social welfare is not something to be given or achieved independently without the invisible hand and the cunning of reason. Hegel's self-consciousness and Adam Smith's self-interest are in essence a theological approach to the human self-conscious desire. In their theology of economic life, the cunning of reason and the invisible hand are not the supplementary tools that are introduced to make up for the limit of human self-conscious desire. It is rather the other way around. Hegel's self-consciousness and Adam Smith's self-interest have their theological origins in the divine providence. Hegel's God is the Wisdom of Reason (*vernunft*) to be realized in the world through development of the human self-conscious desire, and Adam Smith's God is the Wisdom of Nature whose never-failing goodness is embedded in the human desire for self-interest.

By critically comparing their arguments, we may notice that the arguments of Ullmann-Margalit are the result of the emphasis on rational (*vernunftig*) self-consciousness without taking into account the theological foundations, and Davis' arguments are the result of the emphasis on the natural self-interest, as he pays attention to the theological backgrounds. The differences of these arguments are a good example showing that human self-conscious desire has many colours like a rainbow, depending on where we stand. In the theology of economic life, the human self-conscious desire is a way of salvation according to both Adam Smith and Hegel, not in spite of, but because of the invisible hand and the cunning of reason respectively. The invisible hand and the cunning of reason are not the hiding places defying human rational investigation, but stepping stones for the human self-conscious desire that has multiple colours as a way of salvation for individuals and society. Consequently, both the invisible hand and the cunning of reason have similarity and dissimilarity. They are similar not just because both ideas have the same focus on the fact that the human self-conscious desire leads to general welfare by an ultimate design without any individual intention, but also because the human self-conscious desire is God's providence as a way of salvation in the world or in a world to come. In addition, they are different because they stand on different theological foundations, rather than Adam Smith's invisible hand being related to the numerous ordinary humans, and Hegel's cunning of reason to the historical heroes.

In this vein, at the centre of the relationship between the cunning of reason and the invisible hand, there are theological issues about God's identity: Hegel's God is the immanent God of the world with rational providence; Adam Smith's God is the transcendent God over the world with natural providence. If the God of Hegel works through the rational self-consciousness of individuals, which is the providential Wisdom of Reason by which God is to be self-realized in the world, then the God of Adam Smith works though the natural self-interest of individuals, which is the providential Wisdom of Nature by which the transcendent God presides over the world. Therefore, the cunning of reason is the providence of the immanent God who is to be realized through humans. The human self-conscious desire is to be realized in a relationship with others by mutual recognition in the ethical world of the state. The invisible hand is however the providence of the transcendent God who has self-sufficiency and never-failing goodness for humans. The human self-conscious desire is given in human nature as a base for a mutual relationship with others in the natural world of the market.

5.4. Summary and Conclusion

Hegel's cunning of reason is God's divine providence in the world, while the invisible hand is God's divine providence over the world in Adam Smith's theological world. Both Adam Smith's invisible hand and Hegel's cunning of reason are the centre of their theological foundations of economic thoughts, rather than unnecessary or contradictory irony. If God's grace over the world as the theological aspect of Adam Smith's self-interest is closely related to his providential concept of the invisible hand, then God's self-realization in the world as the theological dimension of Hegel's self-consciousness is well expressed in his providential concept of the cunning of reason. The invisible hand is the essence of Adam Smith's theology of economic life. It is his conceptual tool with which to convey his theological belief that there is always a solution and way for salvation in spite of the conflict and tension between the never-failing goodness in God's providence and the human weakness in their fragile nature. The cunning of reason is Hegel's way of dealing with God's providential intervention into the world which is in the process of development by rational (*vernunftig*) self-consciousness in his theology of economic life. It is his conceptual tool with which to convey his theological belief that there is always a solution and way for salvation in spite of the conflict between human nature as evil and human reason as good. Cunning of reason is his theological precept with which to deal with God's wisdom hidden in human economic life that is in constant movement but always in God's providence.

When we turn to the providential aspect of the human self-conscious desire, the role of the invisible hand and the cunning of reason in their system of thoughts is essential and logical rather than unnecessary or irrational. These concepts are closely related to their own understandings of human self-conscious desire and salvation. From the theological foundations of the economic ideas of Adam Smith and Hegel, human weakness is a matter of evil to be overcome for Hegel, and God's grace for Adam Smith. Humans are weak in the sense that they pursue their own limited self-interest. Self-interest is natural in the sense that the desire is given as nature imbedded in human instinct by the wisdom of Nature. Self-interest is therefore not only the proof of human weakness but also of God's goodness as the Creator in Adam Smith's thought. For Hegel, human weakness is to be overcome by ethical life, while Smith believes that human weakness is the natural instinct that cannot be negated by human reason. The gap between what is and what should be is minimized in Adam Smith's thought by accepting human weakness as the goodness of God's providence, while in Hegel, it needs to be transcended by God's self-actualization through the development of human self-consciousness in the world.

In conclusion, Adam Smith's invisible hand and Hegel's cunning of reason are inevitable ideas in their theology of economics to convey the theological dimension of human existence expressed in their approaches to the role of self-conscious desire as a way of salvation. Those expressions fit their system of thoughts respectively to see their theological thoughts. For Adam Smith, God is always good but transcendent over the world, so the invisible hand is the best expression he may choose to explain God's relationship with the world. However, for Hegel, God is neither good nor bad but to be self-realized in the world, so the cunning of reason is the proper language he may use to explain God's relationship with the world. Therefore, from the theology of economics in Adam Smith and Hegel, it is reasonable to conclude that theology and economics are not the matter of either human economy or God's economy. The invisible hand and the cunning of reason are no longer awkward, ironic or inconsistent expressions, but they are God's providence embedded in the theological dimension of self-interest in Adam Smith and Hegel's works respectively. This conclusion helps to achieve the aim of the book to show that economics and theology are interrelated.

CHAPTER 6

Poverty and the State in the Theology of Economics in Smith and Hegel

'Blessed are the poor in spirit, for theirs is the kingdom of heaven' (Matthew 5:3). The sermon on the mountain starts from the vivid and colourful description about the meaning of salvation without losing the concern about the harsh reality of everyday life. It deals with poverty, the spirit, and the kingdom of heaven in a paradoxical way. The aim of this chapter is to investigate the role of the state and poverty for salvation in the theology of economic life in Adam Smith and Hegel's works. Is there any theological reason for why the main thinkers are different in their understandings of the role of state and poverty in relation to salvation? That is the question of this chapter. In the previous chapter, it is shown that those seemingly problematic concepts such as the invisible hand and the cunning of reason cannot be properly understood without the theological dimension of the human self-conscious desire. This chapter will also show that their approaches to economic poverty and the role of the state are based on their own theological foundations.

6.1. Adam Smith's Poverty and Hegel's Poverty

What is poverty and how do we solve it? Poverty is natural in Adam Smith's theology of economic life, while it is not rational (*vernunftig*) in Hegel's theology of economic life. The theological backgrounds embedded in the thoughts of Adam Smith and Hegel lead to different approaches to economic poverty. There is a theological flavour in their understanding of economic poverty. They suggest different solutions to economic poverty as they have different theologies. Different theology leads to different economics.

Poverty is usually assumed as undesirable as it deprives people of not only economic things such as food, clothing, and shelter, but also moral and psychological self-esteem received in the community. Some spiritual people, however, believe that the voluntary renunciation of material goods is a way to salvation. Some believe that the more we have, the happier we will be, but there are also others who believe that the less we have, the happier we will be. Poverty is not just an economic issue but also a moral and theological one as well.

The problem of poverty seems to be beyond our solution as there is no period in human history in which we are rich enough not to have the poor any more. Even in this comparatively affluent society of today, poverty is still the main issue, not only in economics but also in theology. In Adam Smith's thought, happiness does not depend on economic wealth. He says that even 'the beggar, who suns himself by the side of the highway, possesses that security which kings are fighting for'.[1] In contrast, there is a clear conflict between economic poverty and human happiness in Hegel's theology of economic life as he believes that poverty may lead to evil.[2]

In Adam Smith's thoughts, poverty is natural and still in God's providence, while Hegel thinks that poverty is an evil to be overcome. For Hegel, poverty is not an absolute concept; rather, it is relative as he thinks that we feel poor only when compared to others. Hegel believes that poverty is a social evil that alienates the poor from society, religions and even themselves. In Adam Smith's thoughts, however, poverty is not an evil but has a providential purpose that works for human happiness through human self-interest as shown in the story of a deceived son.[3] Adam Smith believes that poverty doesn't necessarily lead the poor to ethical corruption as self-interest is a gift given by the goodness of God who knows human weakness. Adam Smith believes that the vices and follies of humankind are a neces-

1 TMS.IV.I.11.
2 PR 244 Addition.
3 TMS IV.1.8.

sary part of God's providence.[4] Theological precepts lead them to different attitudes to poverty. A theological implication is hidden yet again in their approaches to economic poverty.

In contrast, Hegel's approach to the issue of poverty has three different faces. For him, it is an economic poverty of the poor, caused by mass production without enough consumers; a moral degradation of rabbles, caused by alienation related to economic poverty; religious escape to an otherworldly worldview as a result of losing social unity caused by an economic and moral dimension of poverty. The aim of this section is not in examining the validity of their beliefs, but rather in clarifying what theological precepts lead them to their own economic ideas, if any.

Economic Approach to Poverty

Poverty has an economic aspect. No matter how rich we are, there are always those who are richer than us. This antinomy between wealth and poverty is clearly shown in Hegel's argument that the accumulation of wealth is the direct cause of economic poverty.[5] Poverty and affluence are indivisible in his economic thoughts. This economic idea has a theological flavour in the sense that it is resonant with his theological interpretation of the original sin: God has both the positive and the negative in himself; good and evil are indivisible; we are free to have rational self-consciousness to tell the difference between them. Then in Hegel's perspective we are free to recognize the paradox of the indivisible relationship between affluence and poverty.

To understand his argument, it is helpful to have a look at his explanation of the accumulation process of economic wealth. There is always a tension between nature and reason in Hegel's thoughts, because he believes that the dynamics of the natural desire of humans need to be transcended and preserved. According to his way of thoughts, we as humans cannot

4 TMS I.ii.3.4.
5 PR 245.

stay in nature like animals; we should be free from the shackles of animal nature. In Hegel's words, we must not, even for a moment, imagine that the natural world is of a higher order than the spiritual world.[6] This attitude flows through his description of the process for the accumulation of wealth.

In fact, Hegel fully admits that the commercial market of the civil society has a strong merit in that the dependent reciprocity of work and the satisfaction of individual needs contribute towards the satisfaction of others' needs.[7] This affirmative role of the system of needs as a unifying factor between individual self-autonomy and social communality is not to be left alone; rather, it is to be supplemented by individuals belonging to the estates in civil society. Individuals find it beneficial for their own interest rather than others-interest to have recourse to others in the estates in Hegel's thoughts.[8] However, Hegel is not fully content with the role of the estates or classes although he emphasizes its importance. His uneasiness about the civil society is due to his belief that self-interest is a selfish nature rather than a rational reason. Therefore, he needs a higher ethical life to make the unity of individuals in the civil society firm and solid. That is the role of state in his thoughts as the final moment of the ethical life in which we are not any more independent individuals but complete communal beings. Consequently, natural self-interest and communal welfare are indivisible since individual self-consciousness is realized in the state as the march of the immanent God. This is his idea of the rational state, which is different from the wisdom of God in nature.

However, poverty confronts him in experiential reality, so he tries to find the reason of poverty from the negative side of the commercial market, which he recognizes from the beginning as he approaches the nature of self-interest. Hegel argues that the commercial market of his time has an inherent tendency to produce more than is demanded by consumers when the activity of civil society is unfettered in expansion of its population and

6 PR 272.
7 PR 199.
8 PR 201.

the market.[9] According to Hegel's argument, the development of tools and the division of labour increase not only economic wealth but also social dependence of the class tied to the work. A group of people who belong to the industry that cannot attain enough consumers are to be estranged from the market. Consequently, their specialized labour is no longer a merit but an obstacle against returning back to the market. They are deprived of all the advantages of society such as skills, education, justice, health care, and even religion.[10] They are locked in a vicious circle which cannot be broken by the creation of more jobs for them since the main reason of poverty, for Hegel, is the inevitable overproduction caused by the dynamics of the commercial market composed of the individuals who are concerned with their own self-interest.[11] Despite the excess of wealth, civil society is not wealthy enough.[12] Then, according to his explanation, economic poverty is not an escapable misfortune of individuals who may have a low quality of work skills but an inevitable failure of the commercial market which cannot find enough consumers for the products produced by the unrestricted human desire for self-interest. Hegel's clear outline of the process of poverty is open to the question of whether his argument for the power of the absolute reason in the state against the wisdom of God in nature is proper or not, because his thought about poverty seems to have its origin in his negative attitude against natural self-interest that has a theological colour related to the original sin as mentioned above.

Ethical Approach to Poverty

Poverty has an ethical aspect. Poverty is an evil for Hegel since it is the cause of ethical depravity. In Hegel's ethical life, the individual self-consciousness is to be fully realized in the state in which humans internalise

9 PR 243, 245.
10 PR 241.
11 PR 182.
12 PR 245.

social value and identifies self-interest with it; an individual is born again as a communal being realizing self-consciousness. Hegel believes that poverty for Hegel may break down this connectivity in the modern society. If we are poor below the level of a certain standard of living, in Hegel's thoughts, we lose the feeling of right, integrity, and honour, all of which come from supporting oneself by one's activity and work.[13] According to him, the feeling of loss is not the automatic result of poverty; rather, it is a phenomenon of the modern society like in the England of his time where even the poorest believe that they have their own rights. When the poor are conscious of the rights and feel its loss, they become estranged from the solidarity with inner antagonism against the rich, society and government. Hegel calls these people a rabble, who do not have sufficient honour to gain their livelihood through their own work, yet claim that they have a right to receive their livelihood.

In addition, the difficulty of the ethical side of poverty is in the solution as much as in the cause. Hegel argues that it is contrary to the principle of the civil society and the feeling of personal autonomy to either help the poor through public institutions such as hospitals, foundations and monasteries or subsidise the poor with the money from the taxes on the rich.[14] A direct from of assistance such as charity gives the poor only shame rather than personal autonomy, and creating jobs for them to come back to the workplace is not the solution either. As discussed, the economic side of poverty is not easily solved by creating jobs for them as the economic reason of poverty is caused not by scarcity but by affluence. More jobs will create more affluence, which leads to more poverty according to Hegel's analysis of the economic side of poverty. According to Hegel, the only economic solution is to get rid of overproduced products and to resettle the poor people by colonization.[15] Civil society is driven to establish colonies for a new market and sphere of industrial activity.[16] Hegel believes that there is

13 PR 244.
14 PR 245.
15 PR 248.
16 PR 248 Addition.

no other option but colonization as the only solution to solve the problem of poverty, because colonization helps to secure the raw materials and new markets for overproduced goods and to resettle poverty-stricken people. However, colonization seems to be self-contradiction in Hegel's thoughts because it is against mutual recognition as shown in the master-slave relationship. According to Hegel's logic, we cannot be ourselves unless we recognize ourselves in others who recognize us. Once we colonize others as slaves, then we ourselves lose our identity as there is no mutual recognition. If Hegel's theory is something to be applied only to individuals and the state, but not to international relationships, it does not seem to be rational. Here we may ask two questions about the validity of Hegel's approach to the ethical aspect of poverty: one for the cause of poverty, the other for the solution to poverty.

The first question is whether poverty is the main cause of the moral depravity we experience in experiential reality as Hegel assumes, or whether it is natural. Hegel's argument for poverty as the main reason for an ethical depravity of a rabble is that poverty deprives the poor of all the advantage that members of society have; for example, an ability to acquire necessary skills, education, judicial justice, healthcare and even the consolation of religion. This feeling of loss in their rights makes them a rabble rebelling against the union of society.[17] This may be probability but not inevitability; Hegel is still required to answer why poverty inevitably leads to a moral depravity. If the moral depravity is, as Hegel argues, caused by the relative feeling of loss in their rights they deserve, it is not only the development of human self-consciousness or self-respect as Hegel assumes, but it is also another example of human weakness as Adam Smith assumes. Hegel seems to miss the aspect of the natural weakness of humans while he pays attention to the aspect of rational self-consciousness in the phenomena of ethical depravity. Hegel's self-consciousness of relative loss is quite similar to Adam Smith's explanation of self-interest as the natural feeling of envy and admiration of wealth. In this vein, therefore, there seems to be no direct correlation between a relative feeling of loss and ethical depravity.

17 PR 241.

In addition, Hegel himself admits that our lives do not begin at the same starting line; we are born with natural endowment, physical and mental, which are unequal from the beginning; these inequalities and differences with other circumstances necessarily produce inequalities of wealth and skill.[18] We may then argue that poverty might be a natural phenomenon of everyday lives in human history rather than an abnormal result unique to the commercial market of the modern society. When we consider Hegel's argument that poverty is the relative feeling of loss rather than of the absolute or basic need, it supports our assumption that poverty is a matter of natural instinct rather than a matter of rational reason. In this sense, we may conclude that there is a defect in Hegel's approach to the ethical aspects of poverty. Poverty could be natural rather than the cause of an ethical retardation of a rabble. This is the point of Adam Smith's argument when he says that even the beggar is not God-forsaken as far as the nature of Wisdom is concerned.[19]

One of the problems in Hegel's arguments is in his own theological assumption that there is an insurmountable gap between nature and reason (*vernunft*). He believes that the gap between natural self-interest and rational self-consciousness can be bridged by ethical life and divine providence. However, human passion as the cunning of reason cannot solve the problem of poverty partly because poverty is not rational but natural. There is no room for natural reality in Hegel's logic that the real is rational, and the rational is real. This is the point where Adam Smith's theological dimension of self-interest may be helpful. According to Adam Smith's theological assumptions, the real is natural, and the natural is real. Poverty is natural and still in the Wisdom of Nature. The invisible hand is God's providence in his theology of economics.

The second question is about the validity of Hegel's way of solving the ethical problem of poverty. Hegel's analysis stands on the assumption that humans have undeniable personal autonomy. This rational self-consciousness cannot be denied or deprived even by the institutions of

18 PR 200.
19 TMS IV.I.10.

the state because personal self-consciousness is the only medium through which God is to be realized in the world. The natural self-interest of individuals in the civil society is to be completed and unified firmly in the state which is the earthly divinity for Hegel as it is the march of God in the world.[20] Therefore, for Hegel, this feeling of self-sufficiency and honour in self-consciousness is not to be replaced with any exterior help subsidized by others. Then we may understand why Hegel is so concerned about the value and role of personal autonomy even in the case of the problem of poverty. He accepts his inability to completely solve the problem of poverty although he knows that poverty is the inherent defect in his system of ethical life regardless of whether it is an economic or moral issue. Therefore, his approach to poverty is in essence theological because his faith in the value of the rational self-consciousness of the autonomous individual is related to his theological preconceptions.

Yet again, we need to remember his belief in the difference between natural self-interest and rational self-consciousness. Starting from the premise that there is an insurmountable gap between nature and spirit, Hegel tries to bridge two islands by the development of self-consciousness: reason. That is probably the reason why Taylor ironically calls Hegel a romantic.[21] Just like a romantic tries to find a whole by intuition, according to Taylor, Hegel does the same job by his own reason, which is synthetic reason rather than analytic understanding in Hegel's thoughts. Hegel believes that by synthetic reason we are able to comprehend the essence of the reality. Therefore, he can say that the wisdom of God in nature is the last thing we can imagine since the world of spirit is not the world of nature. Then we cannot either nullify or justify Hegel's argument that poverty cannot be solved in a financial way of helping the poor, since there is no more division between knowledge and faith in Hegel's idea that personal autonomy is the pivotal element of individual self-consciousness not to be replaced with external help.

20 PR 272 Addition.

21 Charles Taylor, *Hegel and modern society* (New York: Cambridge University Press, 1979), 12.

Theological Approach to Poverty

Poverty has a theological aspect in both Adam Smith and Hegel's thoughts. For Adam Smith, poverty is natural and still in God's providence rather than an evil to be overcome by the development of rational self-consciousness. Hegel however believes that poverty is an evil against God's self-realization in the world. We can think of his theological approach to poverty in two aspects: God and human. First of all, we need to remember the discussion about Hegel's God. For Hegel, God is the God of the world immanent in the world to be realized through the development of individual self-consciousness. Then we may assume that Hegel won't accept a poverty-stricken world as the place where God is to be self-realized. Secondly, humans are theologically free to choose between good and evil in the sense that we are like God in our knowledge of good and evil. Then his theological conclusion about poverty will be this: poverty should have no place in the world where God is immanent; otherwise, God's self-realization in the world has no meaning at all since God cannot be the God of the world that is poverty-stricken and ethically depraved. The policy to solve poverty by helping the poor by collecting the taxes from the rich cannot but fail in the end from his theological point of view because rational self-consciousness of self-autonomous individuals is essential for self-realization through which God is to be realized in experiential reality. Therefore, he can conclude that poverty is nothing but an evil in his theological perspective. According to Hegel, poverty is an evil not because it is an economic scarcity, but because it leads to an ethical depravity, so he cannot accept the evil of poverty in the world where God is to be realized.

In Hegel's thoughts, the only way to solve the evil of poverty is by the idea of the state, which is divine will rather than particular states or institutions.[22] In the state, both God and humans are to be realized completely in mutual recognition without losing either the divinity of God or the humanity of humankind: humans in relation to the realization of the immanent God in the world, and God in relation to the self-realization of humans. Then, God, humans, and the world are unified in his theol-

22 PR 270.

ogy in the sense that they are mutually dependent for their realization although God is not equal or reducible to humans and the world as God is providential with his own telos in Hegel. This is Hegel's romantic synthesis in a theological world. A question to think of is then what implications his theological approach to poverty may have in regard to experiential reality such as political and economic life if the divine state is the only answer in his theological perspective.

Hegel's understanding of Abraham, the progenitor of faith in Christianity, is a good example to explore his theology of economic life. In his book *Early Theological Writings*, Hegel describes Abraham's God as the personal God who presides independently over the world in heaven as the lord of Universe.[23] Hegel believes that Abraham's God is not the God of the world but the God in heaven demanding blind obedience and abject worship; there is an insurmountable gulf between the heavenly God and earthly humans. In addition, from Hegel's perspective of freedom, Abraham's life is not free at all. Hegel contrasts rational freedom with natural freedom. Natural freedom is a negative, individual, subjective, particular freedom from the communal society. Such freedom may be natural but not rational as no human can be separated from community. True freedom is only possible in community. Hegel has faith in a beautiful soul living in community. Therefore, in Hegel's theological perspective, Abraham is not, and cannot be a free human without realizing self-consciousness in communal life. In this vein, Hegel's religious reading of Abraham's life is quite clear. We may say, in Hegel's terminology, that Abraham's God is not real if his God is not rational. From Hegel's theological perspective, Abraham is on the wrong track as he tries to be independent by leaving behind both the love of family and the communality of the society to which he belongs, and to be a blind slave by giving up rational self-consciousness. Plant does not suggest any possible weakness of Hegel's own reading of Abraham's way

23 G.W.F. Hegel and T.M. Knox, *Early Theological Writings* (Chicago, Il.: University of Chicago Press, 1948), 187. Translated by T.M. Knox ; with an introduction and fragments translated by Richard Kroner. With the exception of the speech on classical studies, the translations have been made from Herman Nohl's *Hegel's Theologische Jugendschriften* (Tübingen, 1907).

of life although we agree that the ethical and economic picture of Abraham's life concealed in the firm faith of the traditional religion is nicely reinterpreted from the perspective of Hegel's social community.

However, Hegel's evaluation of Abraham's economic and religious life is heavily influenced by his own theological precepts. In spite of the importance of his acute description of Abraham's way of life, he underestimates or negates a simple but important motive of human behaviour, which is also shown in Abraham: Abraham has a natural desire of self-interest. Of course, in Hegel's theological mindsets, there is bifurcation between self-conscious rationality and self-interested instinct; the former is something *to be achieved rationally*, the latter something *to be given naturally*. In Hegel's faith, we are not natural animals but rational humans as our life is the result of the historical process of achieving real freedom by personal self-realization in the ethical community of the divine state; therefore, self-consciousness cannot be something natural in Hegel. However, Hegel's reading of human behaviour is not justified until his theological preconception about God is proved valid in experiential reality of everyday life. This is the reason why we need to have another theological reading of Abraham from the point of self-interest.

As Hegel points out, Abraham starts his journey by leaving behind all his family, his community, and his lands. However, he is not a vagabond without a particular final destination but a traveller with a clear vision for something. That vision is the calling from God who promises that he will bless him so that all people will be blessed through him (Genesis. 12:3). In the eyes of aliens, including Hegel, Abraham looks irrational. However, in Abraham's eyes, God's interest in the salvation of the world and Abraham's interest in God's blessing are interrelated. Abraham leaves behind everything he has, not just because of just self-negation itself but also because of self-interest. According to Hegel's perspective of self-conscious reason, Abraham's circumcision is nothing but another example of cutting himself off from the community. However, according to Adam Smith's perspective of natural self-interest, it may be interpreted as a self-conscious desire not to lose God's promise. In addition, Abraham's obedience to God when he asks him to sacrifice his only son as a burnt offering is another example which cannot be understood in Hegel's rational self-consciousness unless we presuppose that both God and humans are concerned about their own self-interest. Consequently, from the perspective of self-interest, we may say that Abraham's decision to leave Ur of the Chaldeans is perfectly right as he follows his own desire of *self-interest* with a clear vision about the world waiting for him.

Of course, this is not a matter of right or wrong, as Hegel's faith is in a different context from the traditional religion of Christianity. Hegel's intention is to demythologize and find a communal connection of a beautiful soul. However, the point is in whether Hegel's analysis of human behaviour is able to give a valid explanation. Coming back to the issue of poverty, his economic difficulty at the early stages of his journey does not make him ethically depraved against society. Actually, Abraham is very wealthy as God has blessed him in every way (Genesis 24:1).

According to Hegel's theological-economic reading, Jesus has a different image in his eyes, compared to Abraham. In his *Early Theological Writings*, Hegel argues that Jesus is different from Abraham as the former tries to put the relationship between God and humans on the right track by calling God 'father', in which there is an image of God who is with us in the world rather than separate from us, remaining as an infinite other in heaven.[24] In Hegel's view, the relationship between master and slave in Abraham's God is replaced with the relationship of love: God is the father, not the remote master of the Universe. Recognition of each other as father and son is substituted for alienation of the master and slave relationship in Hegel's reading of Jesus' God. Hegel pays attention to God's communal reality in Jesus. Hegel argues that Jesus is not only the son of God but also the son of his time. Jesus' dilemma is that he could either choose to stay in the community and transform the traditional faith, or remain outside to challenge it. However, the former choice would be ineffective as the stifling religious life of Jews would not accept it, and the latter would be meaningless as the Jews would not understand him. Hegel believes that Jesus' mission is a failure as he chooses to be separated from reality and escape into heaven.[25] He argues that this failure deeply affects the fate of Christianity by leaving it with tension between church and state, and heaven and earth.

24 Ibid., 260–265.

25 Ibid., 287.

The beginning of the Sermon on the Mount of the Gospel of Matthew is a good place to discuss the validity of Hegel's argument about Jesus' mission. Jesus says that the poor in spirit are blessed, for the kingdom of heaven is theirs. From Hegel's theological foundations of his economic thoughts, this may be another example of the other-worldly tendency of Jesus disconnecting from the community, which is the reason why Hegel believes that Jesus' mission is a failure. However, Hegel's reading of Jesus' behaviour seems to be heavily influenced by his rational vision of an ideal community for a beautiful soul; he seems to miss the essence of the saying. The rich image of 'the poor in spirit' is open to many different interpretations. However, it is pertinent to assume that ordinary people around Jesus will not fail to catch the meaning of 'the poor in spirit' as long as their experiential reality is poverty, which was quite probable in Jesus' time. If the body is the same life as the soul as Hegel assumes, we may say that economic poverty and spiritual yearning are naturally interrelated to each other. Once ordinary people catch the meaning, then they may feel blessed because it is said that the kingdom of heaven is theirs. Hegel might not agree with the language 'the kingdom of heaven' since his God is the God of the world immanent on earth rather than in heaven. However, the point of Jesus' saying is not in other worldly heaven but in their salvation here and now. The meaning of poverty in Jesus' saying is less resonant with rational self-consciousness but more so with natural self-interest. Consequently, we might say that Hegel seems to misunderstand Jesus' mission. Jesus does not disconnect from the world, nor does he escape into the kingdom of heaven. He stands firmly, even to the point of his death in this world, not for self-realization but for love.

In sum, their approaches to the cause and solution of poverty are not just limited to an economic aspect, but also have ethical and theological implications. For Hegel's theological foundations of economics, the ethical depravity of a rabble is the result of feeling the relative loss of rights they believe they deserve. However, poverty cannot be easily solved by creating jobs or supporting financial service for the rabble, not only because poverty is the systematic failure hidden in the commercial market, but also because the cause of poverty is the accumulation of wealth by self-interest in the market. In addition, personal autonomy is not to be replaced by exterior subsidy as it is the medium through which God is to be realized in the world. Therefore, poverty is an economic, ethical, and theological matter. However, there is a weakness in his thought: it seems to be naive to believe that economic poverty is the cause of economic affluence; economic poverty does not necessarily lead to ethical retardation; natural self-interest seems to play a powerful role in human behaviour as much as rational self-consciousness. One point we cannot miss in Hegel's dealing with poverty is that his ethical approach to human economic behaviour opens the door not only for communism but also for individualism. His ethical analysis of poverty is closely related to communist economics although personal property, for Hegel, is the essential element for realizing self-consciousness, while his firm faith in the realization of self-conscious rationality by the power of human reason is a foundation of mainstream economics although his rationality is not only economic but ethical and theological as well. At the centre of his analysis of economic and ethical poverty, there are theological preconceptions. Poverty is natural in Adam Smith's theology of economic life, while it is not rational (*vernunftig*) in Hegel.

6.2. Adam Smith's State and Hegel's State

Hegel's state is the final stage of the dialectical development of rational self-consciousness, so the role of the state is essential for salvation in his theology of economic life. Adam Smith's state is an institution that needs to support the freedom of natural self-interest because the free market is the way of salvation for individuals and society in Adam Smith. This bifurcation comes from their theology of economic life.

Hegel is a teleological thinker who believes that human history has a providential end which works through the development of human self-consciousness. In his thought, self-interest is a part of human self-consciousness to be preserved as a motive of human behaviour in the market in which economic individuals seek for their own interests without a direct communal concern for others.[26] Despite the selfishness of economic behaviour in the market, it leads to communal welfare by a dialectical movement.[27] Hegel's argument for the socially desirable result caused by individual self-interest is resonant with Adam Smith's self-interest contributing to social welfare. However, the seemingly similar idea commonly shared in both Adam Smith and Hegel in the economic role of human self-interest for the welfare of society does not go very far together in harmony as their approaches to the economic analysis of the cause of economic poverty and the role of the state for social welfare are different to each other, in spite of their seemingly common emphasis on the importance of individual self-interest for social welfare.

When Adam Smith says that the intervention of the state in the market is to be minimized to the necessary level for protection of rational utility-maximising behaviour so as not to interfere with individual self-interest, Hegel comes up with different ideas that self-interest is to be contained in the state which is an earthly divinity far above the physical world of nature.[28] Adam Smith says that the state is necessary only when it does away with the obstacles that might hinder the liberty of individuals so that they pursue freely their own self-interest given by the wisdom of Nature, while Hegel says that the state does not restrict individual freedom; rather, the final ends of individuals are in the state, for the highest freedom consists in the membership in the state, which alone is the absolute power on earth and the march of God in the world.[29] Hegel's arguments then lead us to a basic but important question of why he argues for a strong role of the state although he argues that individual self-interest should be allowed as the most efficient human desire in the civil society.

To answer the question about a role of the state in relation to the individual self-interest, it is necessary to discover the relationship between economics and theology in Hegel's ideas, for his approach to economic behaviour of individuals in the market is, in essence, dependent on his

26 PR 182.
27 PR 199.
28 PR 272 Addition.
29 PR 258 Addition.

ethical perspectives based on a theological origin that this world is in under the providence of God who is, in his thoughts, to be realized through the development of individual self-consciousness. Therefore, self-interest is a good place to start from because it is regarded as the simple but essential human motive in both Hegel's civil society and Adam Smith's market, and because there is a clear difference between them about its role and meaning. It will be argued that their similar but different understandings of self-interest as a way of salvation for individuals and society are closely related to their different theological worldviews regarding humankind, the world and God.

In Hegel's theology of economics, a purely secular and finite state is bad, but the rational and infinite state is good.[30] The economy is contained within an over-arching institutional framework of the state. The role of the state in the economy is one of the fundamental questions in economics and theology. What is the role of the state for the human economy in the market and God's economy in the church?

In Hegel, the state is the completion of history as the final stage in the development of human self-consciousness. God is to be realized in the world as he believes that the state is the march of the immanent God in the world.[31] Therefore, for him, the highest ethical life is to be a member of the state which realizes the true freedom of individuals.[32] As a member of the state, we are no longer self-interested individuals but a communal member with the will to live with others. In this vein, Hegel says that the state is the end of history: the completion of the development of human society through the realization of self-conscious rationality. The state represents and realizes a kind of providential reason that is superior to that of its individuals, but those individuals also realize such reason as actors within the system of needs. As discussed before, Hegel's self-consciousness is in essence theological faith in self-realization of the immanent God in the world through the state in which individuals realize their true freedom. Eternal life is to be achieved in the world here and now rather than

30 PR 270 Addition.

31 PR 258 Addition.

32 PR 260.

in the world to come there and then by the absolute reason of the state. Consequently, according to Hegel, it is in the state that individuals are most fully themselves since the state is the fullest expression of community.

However, he does not have any particular state or particular institutions in mind; instead, he considers the idea, the actual God, in its own right.[33] The state is not an institution but a final moment of the ethical life which is to be achieved in God's self-realization. The state is the final moment of the ethical life by which personal autonomy is fully achieved rather than limited. Here again, Hegel suggests the unity between personal autonomy and social welfare in the ethical life of the state, which is the march of God who is immanent in the world for his own self-realization through the development of the individual self-consciousness which is to be fully expressed in the civil society where the system of needs is at the centre, with other systems that are subsidiary to support the realization of individual self-consciousness. In Hegel, the state is neither a controlling institution nor a mere unity of different individuals which is a just civil society.[34] Consequently, according to him, the state is a self-conscious entity which realizes its own end without sacrificing the full power of personal autonomy in the civil society. The state is a divine will.[35]

The state as a divine will is the rational state which is infinite within itself rather than a bad state which is purely secular and finite.[36] The state is finite in unity with the infinity just as God is. Therefore, patriotism is not a willingness to sacrifice particular individual interest; rather it is a habitual knowledge that the individual interest is preserved and contained in the interest of the state.[37] For Hegel, the state is the completion of the ethical life in which we are truly free with full self-autonomy as a member who realizes self-consciousness in a communal relationship with others. Hegel tries to solve the conflict between self-autonomy and communality through the idea of the state which is the final development of self-consciousness,

33 PR 258 Addition.
34 PR 182 Addition.
35 PR270.
36 PR 270 Addition.
37 PR 268.

the end of history. For Hegel, we are required to live as a self-conscious communal member with rational reason; otherwise, we are to be alienated not only from society and but also from ourselves. To be communal is to be individual. We are to be completely free only as a member of the absolute community without losing our individuality. We are to realize the true self-consciousness of individuals only in the absolute self-consciousness of the state. This is the beautiful soul living in the state.

Hegel's argument is open to the essential question of how to harmonize the paradox between free autonomy and full communality. The state as the final moment of the ethical life has no meaning unless the state is the march of God whose self-realization is to be in the world. In other words, according to Hegel, it is necessary for the system of needs to be upgraded into the ethical life by the development of individual self-consciousness in relation to others by God's immanent providence of self-realization in the world. However, its solution is more from a theological faith in the immanent providence of God who works with the state, rather than from the knowledge of political economy. Although he emphasizes the role of education regarding this matter, Hegel's idea of the beautiful soul with rational reason unifying both the personal concern and communal value perfectly in the state seems to be too optimistic about the experiential reality in general and human economic behaviour in particular. That is the point of Adam Smith's argument in spite of Hegel's persistent criticism against the idea of the wisdom of God in nature.[38] If Hegel says that Adam Smith is an irrational romantic believing in the wisdom of Nature, then Adam Smith would say that Hegel himself is a hopeless romantic falling in love with the impossibility of the power of reason.

In fact, interestingly, both Hegel and Adam Smith have the same idea that human autonomy is to be fully flowered in the commercial market. Both of them agree that personal autonomy is the dynamic motive of human behaviour not only for individuals but also for society. The similarity leads us to the question of why they differ in their conclusions regarding the role of the state for the salvation of individuals and society.

38 PR 272.

There are three reasons to consider. First of all, there is an economic reason, which is the matter of whether the state has a responsibility about the economic poverty of individuals. In Hegel's thought, individuals cannot realize their self-consciousness without the state, which is the most advanced rationality with self-consciousness for Hegel; the state is not just an institute built by men but a self-conscious being; the state as a person has an essential role for individual self-consciousness to achieve their true freedom in the civil society based on self-interest; without the state, there is no true self-consciousness for individuals in the civil society; the state takes care to ensure that the social aspect of individual self-interest in the civil society is solid.[39] Adam Smith would not agree with this line of thought. The state is necessary not to realize or accomplish individual self-consciousness in the civil society, but to sustain and keep natural instinct embedded in individual self-interest in the market. If Hegel says that the state is the base on which individuals can truly be themselves, Adam Smith would say that individuals are the base on which the state can be truly itself. Secondly, there is an ethical reason, which is the issue of whether the state has a responsibility for the ethical degradation of individuals against social unity. The possible answer would be the same as previously stated. Finally, there is a theological reason, which is the matter of whether the state is related to the realization of God and humans in the world. Hegel's answer would be positive since the state is the place where God is to be realized through the development of individual self-consciousness; poverty is the economic and ethical reason for communal disunity. Adam Smith's answer, however, would be negative since God is transcendent; the relationship between God and humankind is through self-interest, which is the wisdom of Nature.

To the question of what the state has to do with individuals, Hegel would answer that the freedom of an individual is something to be realized in the rational self-consciousness by the ethical life; the state positively achieves it. However, Adam Smith would not draw such a conclusion. He believes that the freedom of an individual is something to be given in natural self-interest by the wisdom of Nature; the state passively confirms it.

39 PR 201.

Therefore, the state is the end of history for Hegel, but the loss of desire for Adam Smith. Hegel believes that poverty is the inevitable result to be produced in the market based on individual autonomy, so poverty is not an individual matter but a systematic defect of the civil society. However, the right of the private property for Hegel cannot be negated since it is the essence of economic self-consciousness through which God is to be realized in the world. For Hegel, the state is the final stage of the three moments of the ethical life to transcend this conflict between individual autonomy and communal harmony and preserve the power of human desire of self-consciousness. This is one of the reasons why he needs the state as the march of God.

6.3. Summary and Conclusion

There is a clear difference in understanding the meaning of poverty and the role of the state of its solution between Adam Smith and Hegel. The reality of poverty is not rational to Hegel even though he believes that the real is rational, and it is the reason why there is a contradiction in his explanation of the reason and solution of poverty. It is natural to Adam Smith. At the centre of the difference, there is a theological issue. Adam Smith believes that this world is filled with God's goodness that never fails, so poverty cannot be the matter of evil against God's providence in his theology of economic life. Poverty is natural, and it may contribute to the accumulation of wealth. In addition, humans can still be happy regardless of their economic poverty in his thought. Therefore, the intervention of the state into the commercial market should be limited to the minimum level. Hegel, however, believes that poverty is an evil that makes people ethically degraded. This world is in a constant process of development for completion in his thought. The state is the final stage of the development as he believes that the ethical state is the place for God's self-realization in this world. These observations imply that the economic issue of poverty and the role of the state for its solution is basically a theological issue. Ironically, happiness or salvation is independent of economic situation in Adam Smith's theology of economics, compared to Hegel who believes that the role of the state is essential to overcome the evil of poverty for the salvation of individuals and society.

In conclusion, Adam Smith believes that poverty is natural and in God's providence, so the scarcity of resources cannot be evil in Adam Smith's theology of economics. Hegel believes, however, that poverty is irrational and is to be overcome in God's providence, so the scarcity of material is an evil in Hegel's theology of economics. Adam Smith and Hegel's theology of economics shows that the nature of poverty is not purely an economic issue but essentially a theological issue. Therefore, it is reasonable to conclude that a one-sided approach to poverty without the consideration of the other side easily misleads our understanding of the nature of poverty. The question of what the role of poverty is and how we deal with it is essentially an economic and theological issue. This observation leads us to approach the issue of poverty from the interrelationship between economics and theology, rather than from a purely economic perspective.

CHAPTER 7

Theodicy: Evil and God in the Theology of Economics

The meaning of evil is essentially a theological question as it is fundamentally related to the question of who God is. In previous chapter, it is shown that poverty is not an evil in Adam Smith's theology of economics, compared to Hegel who certainly believes that poverty is an evil to be overcome as it leads to ethical degradation. It is shown that the difference is a matter of the differences in their theological backgrounds. The aim of this chapter is to pay close attention to the question of theodicy from the perspective of human self-conscious desire. It will be shown that there is a quite different interpretation of theodicy between Adam Smith and Hegel. This difference seems to be inevitable as the concepts of God they have are quite contradictory to each other. We may see that different theological presumptions lead to different economic solutions and as a result different ways of salvation from evil.

7.1. Evil and Self-interest

In the world we live in, good and evil exist like day and night in the world. The Bible is also filled with many stories about conflict between good and evil. In Adam Smith's theological world, God is always good and right even though there is pain and sorrow in our daily lives. If God is good and all-powerful, and exists in, through and over the world (Ephesians 4:6), where does evil come from? Evil is too real in our daily lives to be simply ignored as nothing. What is then the meaning of the reality of evil in the world where God rules? This is the problem of theodicy, the ever-lasting question beyond an easy answer. Theodicy is one of the theological foundations of Adam Smith's economic thoughts. We can see Adam Smith's theological landscape of theodicy through the prism of self-interest.

There is an argument that Adam Smith is not so optimistic about the role of natural self-interest for social welfare, for he modifies the account of the teleological nature of self-interest by increasing the scope for human rationality and intervention.[1] Against this approach, there is a theodicy-based approach to Adam Smith's economic thought, arguing that Adam Smith is very optimistic about the role of self-interest for the commercial society, not because he simply ignores the conflict between self-interest and social welfare, but because there is hidden theology in his economic thoughts.[2]

In these approaches, however, there is little attention given to the various colours of Adam Smith's idea of self-interest. An answer to the question of whether Adam Smith's economic thoughts are secular or religious, pessimistic or optimistic, and atheistic or theistic heavily depends on our world-views implicitly assumed in our way of thought. The ambiguity is not because of Adam Smith's problem but because of our failure in recognising his theological foundations of economic thoughts. We may see whatever we want, especially in Adam Smith's economic thoughts as he is an economist, a moral philosopher, and a theologian of his time. Therefore, the point does not seem to be in the matter of the variation or change in Adam Smith's mind regarding the role of human reason in the commercial society. Neither does Adam Smith's theodicy seem to be something limited to the other tier reserved for God. Rather, the providential nature of self-interest is at the centre of Adam Smith's theodicy because self-interest is not only human weakness but also God's gift in Adam Smith's theological foundations of economic thought. Self-interest is the human nature given by God's providence. Adam Smith is optimistic about the role of self-interest

1 James E. Alvey, 'The Hidden Theology of Adam Smith: A Belated Reply to Hill', *European Journal for the History of Economic Thought*, 11/4 (2004), 623–628.

2 Lisa Hill, 'The Hidden Theology of Adam Smith', Ibid. 8/1 (2001), 1–29. Lisa Hill, 'Further Reflections on the "Hidden Theology" of Adam Smith', *European Journal for the History of Economic Thought*, 11/4 (Winter 2004), 629–635.

as a way of salvation for individuals and society, not because he turns a blind eye to the weakness of the self-conscious desire, but because he has a theological faith in God's theodicy through self-interest.

Adam Smith argues that the vices and follies of humankind are necessary parts of God's plan for the happiness of the whole.[3] He believes that evil exists in the world as a part of the providential process for the salvation of the whole. From his own theodicy, he is able to be optimistic about the human future in spite of weak reason and unstable passions in humans, because he has faith in God's providential benevolence. According to his eschatology, our happiness in this life depends on the humble hope of life to come deeply rooted in human nature. He believes that true happiness is therefore not in the vanity that is just an efficient cause in the transient world, but the ease and tranquillity that are the great and ultimate objects of all our desires in the world to come. He is optimistic about humankind's future in spite of his hesitation of the role of human reason and virtue, because he has faith in God's providential theodicy in which evils are not the end but are used as a process of God's plan for the world to come. Self-interest is the human nature given by God's providence; therefore, it is at the centre of his understanding of theodicy in his teleology and eschatology.

If we see from the prism of self-interest the relationship between good and evil in Adam Smith's theological foundations of economic thoughts, we may get a clear picture of theodicy in his works. There seems to be a conflict in his arguments regarding vanity. He says that it is vanity or pleasure, not ease, which interests us, while he mentions that vanity of self-love is not the ultimate object of our desires.[4] According to his beliefs, God rules over the world, and self-interest is an efficient cause for God's economy of the world. In his thoughts, self-interest in desire of vanity is not the final end, but a part of God's providential plan to deal with the vices and follies of humankind. Self-interest is endowed as an efficient cause by God's providence for the happiness of the whole, and the happiness in this world is dependent on the humble hope and expectation of a life to come, where we are with God in ease and tranquillity without vanity.

3 TMS I.ii.3.4.

4 TMS I.iii.2.1; TMS VII. ii.2.11.

Adam Smith has a broader picture of religious faith in his mind to observe the reality of the daily lives of ordinary humans who are believed to be in constant conflict between vices and virtues consciously or unconsciously. He believes that self-interest is neither a blind selfishness of human autonomy nor a virtuous passion working always properly, but an effective cause for God's ruling over evils. The traditional dichotomy between vices and virtues are synthesized through the providential nature of self-interest for the final cause of procreation and preservation.

The human desire of happiness in this life is 'thus, on many occasions, dependent on the humble hope and expectation of a life to come.'[5] Adam Smith's self-interest is not to be used as a clue for the possibility of the human autonomy by rational reason without God; rather, Adam Smith defines his self-interest as a benign wisdom of God's providence. He does not lose the teleological dimension of the human future in spite of the autonomous self-interest of humans; rather, his self-interest originally comes from the benevolent Nature whose providential telos works for humans through the immanent self-interest given to humans by the deity.[6] Then, self-interest is a tool for God's ruling over the world. Humans are endowed the desire of self-preservation, which is not entrusted to human reason but to the human nature of bettering our condition. God is always good and all-powerful but allows evil. God allows the vices and follies of humankind, because they are necessary parts of God's plan for the happiness of the whole. Evil and sin exist; however, God rules through self-interest. Theodicy is one of the theological foundations of his economic thoughts, and the providential nature of self-interest is at the centre of Adam Smith's theodicy.

5 TMS III.ii.33.
6 TMS I.ii.3.4.

7.2. Sin and Self-interest

Sin is another theological foundation of his economic thoughts, which we can see through the prism of Adam Smith's self-interest. Self-interest is not sin but a way of salvation for individuals and society in Adam Smith's theology of economics. He believes that self-interest is not human sin but God's grace. For him, sin is not self-interest; rather it is self-negligence. If sin is, as generally assumed, a matter of a deficiency, a limitation, a lack of capacity, then it may be true that economic scarcity is sin or evil.[7] However, for Adam Smith, sin cannot be a matter of scarcity since he believes that God's goodness never fails. In his theology of economics, scarcity and poverty are not evil, but God's providence just as affluence and wealth are not good, but a kind of vanity. Consequently, for him, self-interest is not sin, but it is rather God's grace just as others-interest is not human virtue, but God's wisdom. Adam Smith has a theological faith that God gives ample provisions for remedying many of the bad effects of the folly and injustice of man caused by narrow self-love.[8]

Let's have an imaginary experiment, applying self-interest to a story in the Bible. There is a beautiful story in the New Testament about a woman who sinned (John 8: 3–8). In this story, we can imagine the relationship between sin and self-interest from the perspective of Adam Smith's theological foundation of his economic thoughts. 'If anyone of you is without sin, let him be the first to throw a stone at her'. This is the answer given to the people who caught a woman in the act of adultery and used it as a trap. At this answer, those who heard began to go away one by one until only Jesus was left, with the woman still standing there. This story is short but has a profound implication in understanding the meaning of sin and how

7 Vivian Charles Walsh, *Scarcity and Evil* (A Spectrum Book, S-12; Englewood Cliffs, NJ: Prentice-Hall, 1961). A.M.C. Waterman, 'Economics as Theology: Adam Smith's Wealth of Nations', *Southern Economic Journal*, 68/4 (2002), 907–921. Albino Barrera, *God and the Evil of Scarcity: Moral Foundations of Economic Agency* (Notre Dame, IN.: University of Notre Dame Press, 2005).

8 WN IV.ix.28.

to deal with it. Once we understand the three dimensions of self-interest, this short story may give us a profound implication about the way of human existence. We can see a different picture if the scene is shown through the prism of self-interest.

Looking at the scene from the perspective of Adam Smith's theological foundations of economic thoughts, it is natural to assume that the reason they went away is not because they loved Jesus or the woman, but because they behaved according to their own natural desire of self-interest. In other words, those who accused the woman left the place not because they learned human virtue or others-interest but because they were awakened to their own self-interest and sympathy based on it. Jesus' answer after a brief silence led them to see their own self-consciousness, the natural instinct innate in human beings by God's providence, and pinpointed the heart of the issue: *sinful self*. At this, people had no choice but to respond to it with the motive of their own *self-interest* because they noticed that the answer was not only for the woman but actually for the people who caught her. Once they were awakened to the natural self-interest, they felt *sympathy*, which is the moral dimension of self-interest. Subsequently they knew that humans were all sinners to be delivered from evil, which is the theological dimension of self-interest. They then went away one at a time, the older ones first. Consequently, if we approach the story from Adam Smith's theological foundations of economic thoughts, the human desire of self-interest is the central motive of the human behaviour in the story. From this, we may confirm that self-interest is not sin but God's gift in Adam Smith's theological foundation of economic thoughts. Self-interest cannot be simply identified as a sinful nature, but it is a way of salvation for individuals and society. This observation of the role of self-interest needs to be emphasized as it could be a clue to illuminate how and why the theological dimension of self-interest is neglected and even erased in modern theology.

7.3. Adam Smith's Evil and Hegel's Evil

What is evil, and what is good? The matter of good and evil is an everlasting question defying a simple answer. We cannot exactly say what good is unless we clearly define what evil is, and vice versa. In economics, it is generally assumed that abundance is good, so scarcity is evil to be overcome. An economic human is required to efficiently maximize one's own utility to overcome the scarcity of materials. Economic efficiency is the guiding light to recognize good from evil in economics. In theology, however, the difference between good and evil is not in the matter of material affluence or scarcity but is related to the matter of moral behavior and religious faith. It is good to love others and have faith in God, while it is evil to hate one's neighbour and disobey God. It is undeniable that economics and theology seem to approach the matter of good and evil from completely different perspectives, so it seems to be impossible to communicate with each other without changing our assumptions. To have a meaningful conversation of the matter of good and evil, it is necessary and important to ascertain the theological foundations of economic ideas and the economic aspect of theological thoughts, because the matter of good and evil is not just physical but moral and religious as well.

In Adam Smith's theology of economic life, evil does not seem to be a matter of the natural instinct of self-interest or economic scarcity, as he believes that human self-conscious desire is the providence of God whose goodness never fails. Even the vices and follies of humankind cannot be evils to be erased but a necessary part of God's providence in his theology of economic life. Hegel's evil, however, is related to original sin which, he argues, is related to human nature as his theology of economics stands on the preconception that this world is in constant movement for perfection, overcoming human natural instinct by rational (*vernunftig*) self-consciousness. In his book *Hegel and Christian Theology*, Hodgson also argues that evil is a matter of a failure in spiritualization.[9]

9 Peter Hodgson, *Hegel and Christian theology: a reading of the Lectures on the philosophy of religion* (New York: Oxford University Press, 2005), 39.

The bifurcation in understanding evil is shown again in the difference of Adam Smith and Hegel. This difference comes from their theology of economic ideas. In Adam Smith, natural self-interest is a way of salvation, while a rational self-consciousness is a way of salvation in Hegel. Adam Smith believes that human reason is feeble, while Hegel believes that human nature is sinful. The confession of St Paul's confession of his own weakness is a good example. He says that nothing good lives in his sinful nature for he has the desire to do good, but he does the evil he does not want to do (Romans 7: 18–19). In contrast to his frustration in his weakness, however, he also delights in his weakness for he believes that he is strong when he is weak through hardships and difficulties (2 Corinthians 12:10). His delight in weakness in spite of sinful nature comes from his faith that God's grace is sufficient for him, for God's power is made perfect in weakness (2 Corinthians 12:9). From this paradoxical confession, we may imagine a picture of the human condition in reconciliation among evil, good, sin, weakness, perfection, and grace. Taking into account our experiential reality filled with harsh competition in a battlefield of good and evil, his confession is as pertinent in our time as it was in his time. According to Hegel, the superiority of Christianity is in its doctrine that humankind is evil by nature: the doctrine of original sin.[10] Ironically, Hegel continues to argue in the same paragraph that Christianity is the religion of freedom not in spite of, but because of original sin. Then the question is how to discover an equilibrium or reconciliation between good and evil, weakness and perfection, sin and grace, and in an economic language, scarcity and affluence.

In Hegel's thought, humans are by nature evil rather than good as we have original sin. However, Hegel's point of argument is not in sinful nature itself but in the human desire of self-consciousness to be free from sinful nature for we are like God in our knowledge of good and evil.[11] That is the reason why he believes that Christianity is the religion of freedom; more specifically speaking, Christianity has an inherent possibility of being the religion of freedom if we comprehend it properly. By putting human sinful-

10 PR 18 Addition.
11 PR 139 Addition.

ness as evil in sharp conflict against freedom, he is able to argue that human nature is an evil we should escape from for true freedom in human spirit; in addition, we are able to do so since we are like God in our knowledge of good and evil. However, the conflict of evil and good is not only a human problem, but it is also the problem of God in Hegel's thoughts, since he cannot explain where the origin of evil starts unless God has in himself both the positive and the negative. With this theological assumption, Hegel may argue that human self-realization is intertwined with God's self-realization. 'Then you will know the truth, and the truth will set you free' (John 8:32). The more we are by nature evil, the more the role of self-conscious rationality is emphasized for freedom. If we colour the theological language of evil and freedom in Hegel's thoughts with economic language, we can see a clear picture in our experiential reality: economic affluence is freedom and good; economic scarcity is sinful nature and evil.

Hegel's rational self-consciousness that overcomes the evil in the world is different from St Paul's delight that comes from the power of God working through his weakness rather than his strength. According to Paul' belief, we cannot escape our weakness which is in a sense natural, but are able to be perfect with God's grace, which is sufficient to fill the gap between weakness as evil and perfection as good (2 Corinthians 12:9). Weakness and perfection coexist in the experiential reality of St Paul compared to Hegel's emphasis on the self-conscious rationality by which he argues we must not imagine that the weakness of human nature is equal to or higher than the strength of the human spirit.[12] Hegel leaves no room for compromise between human nature and human spirit in human behaviour. If St Paul says that we are strong in our weakness by God's grace, then Hegel will say that we become strong only by transcending the natural weakness in the world where God is to be realized. There are delicate differences between their views about God, humankind, and the world. Considering these differences, let us come back to the economic human in mainstream economics to see if there is any clue to find out some relationship between economics and theology.

12 PR 272 Addition.

Interestingly, modern economics is generally believed to have its origin from Adam Smith who in fact has very different worldviews about God, humans, and the world. Hegel also has both similarities to and differences from the arguments of mainstream economics which is based on an economic human. Hegel believes that social evil is the result of economic poverty, for it leads the poor to feel frustrated with the feeling of relative loss of their civil rights they think they deserve, and this frustration leaves room for ethical depravity against society. However, Hegel's understanding of the reason and result of poverty is different from modern economics in three aspects: firstly, poverty is not the result of individual irrationality, but because of the inevitable failure of the market system; secondly, poverty itself is actually not an evil, but it becomes evil when the poor feel the relative feeling of loss compared to others, and fall into a rabble; thirdly, poverty therefore is not to be solved by economic affluence as assumed in mainstream economics as the market only makes it worse, but to be solved by the final moment of the ethical life, that is, the state where personal autonomy and communal value are to be achieved without humiliation of the poor and arrogance of the rich.[13] Most of all, in Hegel, scarcity as evil is not just a matter of economic materials; rather, it is a personal matter as a communal member, which is to be solved only by development of self-consciousness in relation to others in the communal society. If we assume that an economic human in mainstream economics has come of age in Hegel's state, then we may say that the economic rationality of an economic human in economic liberalism is equal to the self-conscious rationality of a spiritual human in Hegel's thoughts. In spite of these similarities and differences, they both seem to believe that we are strong enough to be able to transcend both the weakness of humans by rationality and the evil of scarcity by good of affluence.

However, Adam Smith would not approach negatively human weakness and scarcity. Firstly, for Adam Smith, human weakness is not something negative to be replaced with reason as in Hegel. He has at the centre of his thoughts a *natural human* who behaves according to inherent self-interest

13 PR 244.

to be given by the wisdom of Nature, rather than a *rational human* who is required to behave according to rationality *to be achieved* by human reason. There is no guarantee that Adam Smith's natural human behaves with economic rationality. For Adam Smith's thoughts, the natural human falls easily into irrational passions as humans are *weak* in rational ability. In contrast to Hegel's God who has both the positive and the negative in himself, Adam Smith believes, however, that the goodness of God never fails despite human weakness. Consequently, the human weakness is God's grace by which a human is strong when he is weak.

According to Hegel's theology of economics, the scarcity of economic resources could be evil to society as it is the reason of ethical retardation of the poor. The deficiency in the private and public sectors is inevitable because the people are alienated by the systematic failure of the market which creates wealth and poverty at the same time. So it is necessary to let the market create economic wealth freely but with a clear vision of economic justice to be achieved only by the supplementary intervention of the state. Adam Smith, however, would say that poverty is not such an evil to be overcome by the ethical state intervention. The state intervention may open the door to the systematic evil at the sacrifice of individual self-interest which is not only human weakness but also God's grace as well. The intervention of the state is not the desirable end of human history but the loss of the dynamics of human desire.

In contrast, Adam Smith believes that poverty is not necessarily evil. He is concerned with the wealth of nations; however, this does not necessarily mean that poverty is evil in his thoughts, for he believes that poverty is a motive for people to work for wealth and respect the rich, which leads to social stability, and that the poor are left no worse off by the wisdom of Nature than the rich as far as the real happiness of human life is concerned.[14] Theological perspective is permeated in his economic thought about poverty and wealth. This is the economic, moral, and theological context in which Adam Smith's concept of self-interest is to be understood.

14 TMS IV.I.10.

Hegel's analysis of the human weakness is different from Adam Smith's. For Hegel, human weakness is to be overcome by ethical life, while Smith believes that human weakness is the essence of a human being which cannot be negated in this world. The gap between what is and what should be is minimized in Adam Smith's idea by accepting human weakness as the goodness of God's providence, while in Hegel, it is to be transcended by God's self-actualization through human self-consciousness in the world. Humans are weak in the sense that they pursue their own limited self-interest. Self-interest is natural in the sense that the desire is given as nature embedded in human instinct by the wisdom of Nature. Self-interest is not only the proof of human weakness but also of God's goodness as the Creator.

7.4. Summary and Conclusion

Poverty and economic scarcity are not evils in Adam Smith's theology of economic life. The self-conscious desire is innate instinct embedded in human nature given by God's providence in Adam Smith' theology, so it cannot be a sin against God in his thought. This world is created by God who is always good, almighty and perfect. Therefore, economic scarcity cannot be an evil in Adam Smith's thought. Poverty and economic scarcity may have their own roles for human welfare through the human self-conscious desire in God's providence. From Hegel's perspective, scarcity itself is not evil but becomes evil when the poor are conscious of the feeling of relative loss in their civil rights. According to Adam Smith's idea, scarcity or poverty is not evil for it works for the creation of wealth and stabilisation of society by self-interest.

CHAPTER 8

Eschatology

If theodicy is about the problem of good and evil in the present world, eschatology is about the end of things. What is an afterlife? Is this world eternal or transient? Is there hell or heaven? All these questions are the issues related to eschatology. A purely theological discussion of those topics in detail is however beyond the limited scope of this chapter. Its main concern is to show that the present-oriented eschatology of Hegel and the future-oriented eschatology of Adam Smith are respectively related to their own theology of economics, and that human self-conscious desire is the strongest motive in their understanding of the end of things. Discussing some eschatological issues such as eternality and afterlife, we will try to find a theological link connecting economic desire with eschatological faith in their theology of economics. By doing so, this chapter will support the argument that economics and theology are interrelated even in an eschatological dimension.

8.1. Self-interest and Eternality

Humans are self-conscious beings, so they have a natural desire for an eternal life whether they are religious or not. What is eternal life? How can we have it? Those questions are always in the human mind even though we may not recognize it. The undeniable finitude of human existence is the base for our concern and desire for eternality. This issue is an ever-lasting question beyond a simple answer just like the existence of evil and good. This section confines the discussion to the relationship between self-interest and eternality. The aim of this section is to explore from the theological dimension of self-interest the difference and similarity between Adam Smith and Hegel in their approaches to the nature of eternality. It will show that human self-conscious desire is closely related to eternality in Adam Smith and Hegel's theology of economics.

Eternality is a theological question and seems to have nothing to say about economic behaviour in the market. However, it is not so simple, because it is also true that an economic human who works hard and saves money has a desire not only for his own better life in the future but also for the happiness of his children and generations to be followed as well. How to understand an eternal life is inevitably related to how to live in the present. This could be an example of the interrelationship between theological faith and economic behaviour. This interrelationship is shown in the approach to eternality of Adam Smith and Hegel. Eternal life is in this world according to Hegel, while it is in a world to come according to Adam Smith. Hegel believes that this world is eternal, compared to Adam Smith who believes that this world is transitory.[1]

This seems to be an irony when we consider the fact that Adam Smith is generally hailed as the father of capitalism where material satisfaction seems to be the ultimate end of life in this world. In Adam Smith's theology of economics, eternality is surely an important dimension of human life, but it is not in this world that is full of vanity. This world is not the final destination but is a finger pointing to the world to come. Then, the question is why they are different in understanding the meaning of eternality even though both of them believe that eternality is an essential element of human life. Is there any theological reason to explain the difference? This world is eternal in Hegel as it is the place where God is to be realized. However, this life and world is transient and transitory, compared to the world to come according to Adam Smith who believes in God's transcendence. The difference in the doctrine of God may explain another clear difference between Adam Smith and Hegel in their belief in eternal life. Adam Smith's eternal life is a matter of a life to come in the future, but Hegel's eternal life is a matter of a life in the present world.

1 PR preface p. 20. TMS IV.1.8. TMS III.2.33.

For Hegel, the world is the place where God's self-actualization through individuals' self-consciousness happens. The end of the world is the actualization of God's self-consciousness by the realization of human self-consciousness. His eschatology is circular in the sense that God actualizes himself through human self-consciousness, and humans realize themselves through God's self-consciousness. For him, God and humans are one and the same in the realization of self-consciousness in his eschatology; therefore, this world is not transient but eternal as the place for self-realization of both human and God. For Adam Smith, however, the world is the place where we stay temporarily with the hope that there is a world to come. He believes that our happiness in this life is dependent upon 'the humble hope and expectation of a life to come: a hope and expectation deeply rooted in human nature.'[2]

In Adam Smith's thoughts, self-interest is a way of salvation not only for individuals but also for society as sympathy is a principle of human relationships based on natural self-interest which is not selfish blindness but the providential wisdom of Nature imbedded in human instinct as God's providence for human happiness both in the world and in a life to come; however, Hegel suggests rational self-consciousness as a way of salvation for both individuals and society as the mutual recognition is the principle of human relationship based on rational self-consciousness, which is not naturally given but rationally achieved in the ethical life in the community. At the centre of the difference, there is a theological issue.

8.2. Self-interest and Afterlife: Heaven and Hell

In the previous section, we examine the similarities and differences in Adam Smith and Hegel's approaches to eternality. Naturally, the subsequent question is about the issue of afterlife. Is there an afterlife or a life

2 TMS III.2.33.

to come? If so, what about heaven and hell? Do Adam Smith and Hegel believe in their existence? What do they say about the reality of heaven and hell in their theologies of economics? That is the question. In this section, it will be shown that the theological aspect of human self-conscious desire is an important key to understand the meaning of an afterlife in Adam Smith and Hegel.

Adam Smith is a theologian who has faith in a divine providence presiding over the world. God's goodness never fails in this world or in a world to come in his theology of economics. Then, it is natural for him to have faith in the afterlife or a life to come.[3] His point is however not in a life to come itself. His main concern is that self-interest is still the strongest motive of moral behaviour in this world and for religious faith in a world to come. He believes that we are always conscious of God and acting in front of him. This human self-consciousness is the theological aspect of self-interest that is a gift from God for human weakness.[4] Adam Smith has strong faith in the importance of afterlife. However, he is not so much concerned about hell as he is about heaven. God's goodness never fails in his theology. The world to come is the place where God's goodness will reward the just rather than the place where the wicked will be punished. A life to come is explained in relation to heaven without mentioning hell.[5]

This tendency of hesitating to use the language hell is shown again in the sentence that was added in the 6th edition of his work. He says, 'in every superstition that the world has ever beheld, accordingly, there has been a Tartarus as well as an Elysium; a place provided for the punishment of the wicked, as well as one for the reward of the just.'[6] In the passage, we may feel that hell and heaven are mentioned not exactly in the meaning of Christian orthodox belief, but in the context of religion and superstition. Adam Smith does not clearly say that the idea of hell is superstitious or unnecessary. However, it is important to pay attention to his word choice. He does not use the language of hell, which is a Christian concept, but

3 TMS III.5.12.
4 TMS III.5.12.
5 TMS III.5.10.
6 TMS II.ii.3.12.

mentions Tartarus, a term generally used in Greek mythology. In addition, the Christian concept of hell is never mentioned either in the book or in his other main works. Compared to his hesitation to use the word hell, heaven is used in his works as the place we appeal to God's justice.[7]

Then the question is: is there any reason why Adam Smith prefers to use the language of heaven to the expression of hell in explaining the meaning and role of the afterlife in his theology of economics? Before we answer this question, we need to pay attention to the introduction of *TMS*, where Raphael and Macfie point out important changes in the 6th edition of *TMS*, arguing that Adam Smith moves away from orthodox Christianity to natural religion, although he is still religious without following Hume into scepticism.[8] The important doctrinal concepts of orthodox Christianity such as revelation and atonement are replaced with pagan terms such as Tartarus (hell) and Elysium (heaven) in the passage of II.ii.3.12. In addition, the long discussion of orthodox Christian doctrines regarding God's holiness and the necessity of atonement shown in the previous edition is suppressed into a short sentence, which is a plain description about religion and superstition without using any specific Christian terms. The possibility of Adam Smith's change of attitude in his Christian belief is discussed in detail again in the Appendix II of *TMS*.[9]

Then, it may be true that Adam Smith is not in favour with orthodox Christian doctrines in general, and, atonement and revelation in particular. It could also be true that Adam Smith's quote of Voltaire's satirical couplet on the Christian concept of hell is an example to show that Adam Smith moves away from orthodox Christianity to natural religion. From all these observations, it seems be partly reasonable to conclude that he tries to move away from orthodox Christianity by erasing the Christian undertone in his work. His moving away from orthodox Christianity could then explain why he prefers to use the language of heaven to the expression of hell when he explains the afterlife.

7 TMS IV.I.8.
8 TMS p. 19.
9 TMS p. 400.

However, the argument of this section is slightly different. In my opinion, those observations seem to miss the point Adam Smith tries to convey in his theology of economics even though they are well supported based on the important changes in the 6th edition of *TMS*. As discussed in the section dealing with Adam Smith's theological background in chapter 2, his negative attitude is not towards Christianity itself but to superstition and fanatic enthusiasm. His warm and affirmative attitude towards the Protestant churches is well expressed in his work.[10] The point is therefore not whether he moves away from orthodox Christianity or not, but what kind of faith is embedded in his theology of economics, for there are many different kinds of Christian faiths not only in his time but also today. It would then be reasonable to see if there are other logical and natural reasons why he hesitates to use the expression of hell, and erases the expressions such as atonement and revelation in the 6th edition of *TMS*.

In this section, a different approach is taken by paying attention to the theological aspect of human self-conscious desire. Self-interest is an important link we should consider to connect economic ideas with religious thought in Adam Smith's theology of economics. Unfortunately, the theological dimension of Adam Smith's self-interest is not taken into consideration in the arguments of Raphael and Macfie.[11] Adam Smith does not confine divine salvation to religious life. Rather, he extends it to even everyday life through his idea of self-interest. Self-interest is still the strongest motive in the human desire for an afterlife in his theology of economics. Therefore, the point is not whether he is an orthodox Christian or not, but in how he uses the concept of self-interest to convey his theological ideas regarding the afterlife. As discussed in chapter 2, God's never-failing goodness and human weakness as grace are his theological foundations on which he builds up the theological dimension of human self-conscious desire. This gives us a clue to explain why he hesitates to use the language of hell, and omits theological jargon such as atonement and revelation.

10 WN V.i.g.41.

11 Raphael and Macfie, Appendix II of TMS p. 400.

It is natural and logical for Adam Smith to prefer heaven to hell in explaining the afterlife. For Adam Smith, self-interest is natural instinct given by God's providence whose goodness never fails in this life or in a life to come. God's never failing goodness and benevolence is the theological foundation of his economic ideas. Therefore, it is reasonable for him to evade the use of the language of hell and use the word of heaven. Heaven as the place of eternal hope is a more convenient and proper concept than hell as the place of eternal punishment for him to explain God's providence. His strong faith in the transcendent God whose goodness never fails fits well with heaven, rather than with hell.

In this vein, Adam Smith's evading theological jargon such as atonement and revelation is reasonable in his theology of economics. In chapter 5, it is shown that the invisible hand is a theological link connecting human self-conscious desire with God's providence over the world in Adam Smith's theology of economics. As long as the afterlife is an extension of human desire into the world to come, it is not just a matter of a theological issue but also a matter of an economic one in his thought. It is then reasonable for him to use self-interest to explain the nature and meaning of the afterlife. Therefore, there is no need for him to use theological jargon such as atonement and revelation in explaining the afterlife, for he has the theological link of self-interest as the strongest motive even in a world to come. In this sense, the change in the 6th edition does not necessarily mean that he moves away from his Christian faith. It is logical and natural for him to omit the passage on atonement and revelation, and substitute it with the general sentence without Christian undertones. Theological concepts such as atonement and revelation are neither negated nor simplified, but economised in his theology of economics. The theological dimension of self-interest is the strongest motive even for the afterlife in his theology of economics.

Contrasted with Adam Smith, Hegel's theology of economics has quite a different approach to the afterlife. We have discussed in chapter 3 that human self-conscious desire is a way of salvation for Hegel as for Adam Smith. However, Hegel does not believe in, or more specifically, has no necessity of assuming the existence of afterlife. Firstly, Hegel's God is not the transcendent God as in Adam Smith. His God is neither all-powerful nor always good, but a self-realizing entity in the world through the development of rational human self-consciousness. God is here in this world, so there is no need to assume a life to come in Hegel's theology of economic life. Secondly, this world is eternal for Hegel, compared to Adam Smith who believes that this world is transient, so he believes that it is mere vanity to look for an afterlife beyond this world. His present-oriented thought has no choice but to deny an afterlife. Finally, there is no clear distinction between evil and good in Hegel's theology of economics. Therefore, he does not need such an afterlife as the place of reward for the good and punishment for the evil. Hegel is a teleological thinker. He has faith in providential ends of human history culminating towards the apex in the state. The cunning of reason is a part of God's self-realizing process through the development of rational self-consciousness until God and humans achieve self-realization in the world. Therefore, it is reasonable for him to have faith in the ethical life in this world, not an afterlife in the world to come.

8.3. Self-interest and the Kingdom of God

When we talk about eschatology, the issue of the kingdom of God is another important topic frequently discussed in theology along with eternality and afterlife. They are similar eschatological issues, but have different angles of perspective. If the issue of eternality is a concern about the transient aspect of human existence, the afterlife is about the place of heaven and hell. Compared to these eschatological dimensions of human life, the kingdom of God is mainly related to God's ruling in, over and through the world, rather than a specific realm or time. The main concerns of this section are however limited to a brief comparison of the nature of the kingdom of God in Adam Smith and Hegel's theology of economics. Two main points are discussed: one is about the range of the kingdom of God; the other is about an economic dimension of the theological issue of the kingdom of God.

The Range of the Kingdom of God

The phrase 'Kingdom of God' is never used in Adam Smith's main works, nor is it used in Hegel's *Philosophy of Right* except in one case when he compares the church and the state, arguing that emotional religion itself should not hold the reins of government which belongs to the rational state. Hegel uses the language of the Kingdom of God in a negative context, and we may understand his position when we take into account that the state is the divine providence of God in the world. In Hegel, there is no kingdom of God without the state which is the present spirit of divine will. The point we can think of is the range of the kingdom of God.

Adam Smith's kingdom of God has two tiers, one is this transient world and the other is the eternal world to come. In his kingdom of God, God is invisible and hidden in this world of illusion that is full of vanity, but real in the world to come. Hegel's kingdom of God however is real and eternal in this world.

In Hegel's thought, there is no idea of a life to come. For him, the supreme manifestation of realization of God is in the state; therefore, the kingdom of God based on religious feeling or emotion is required to give way to the rational state. In addition, in Hegel's Kingdom of God, there is no room for people who are regarded as natural or irrational, for example, children, women and other ethnic groups. Inevitably, we may conclude that Hegel's kingdom of God might be concrete in the state but very narrow in its range.

Compared to Hegel's Kingdom of God, Adam Smith's Kingdom of God seems to be broader than Hegel's despite the fact that he never uses the language in his main works. If we understand the meaning of the kingdom of God roughly as the world that God rules over, Adam Smith has two kinds of Kingdom of God compared to Hegel: in this world and in the life to come. In this world, the essence of the kingdom of God is God's grace. Adam Smith describes that our world is filled with the goodness of God, for every part of nature equally demonstrates the providential care of its Author even in the weakness and folly of humans.[12] In Adam Smith's Kingdom of God, no one is forlorn outside of the Kingdom of God. He believes that God rules with unfailing goodness.

'Let the little children come to me, and do not hinder them, for Kingdom of God belongs to such as these' (Mark 10:14). This is one of the many biblical stories related to the kingdom of God. One thing we may assume from the parable is that there is more significance in the weakness of human nature rather than the power of human reason. This is shown again in another biblical story as follows. 'The wolf will live with the lamb, the leopard will lie down with the goat, the calf and the lion and the yearling together; and a little child will lead them' (Isaiah 11:6). Of course, the meaning of the verses is a hermeneutical issue. However, it gives a feeling about the biblical description of the kingdom of God. More interestingly, the range of biblical salvation does not seems to be limited to humans, but also includes the whole of creation, because the whole creation has been groaning in hope that all of creation itself will be liberated from its bondage to decay and brought into salvation (Romans 8:21–22).

The difference between Adam Smith and Hegel may be explained by their theology of economics. Hegel's kingdom of God seems to be something to be achieved in the world by the development of our self-conscious rationality. Hegel's main concern is to explain how to achieve the kingdom of God in this world, so he has no choice but to have faith in the power of human reason to be realized with God's immanence. In Adam Smith, the Kingdom of God is something to be given to the world by the wisdom of Nature in our hope for a life to come where true happiness is to be achieved; therefore, he is at ease with human nature in this kingdom of God until we reach the life to come. The Kingdom of God is always perfect as it is regardless of human weakness or wisdom in Adam Smith's theology of economics, while it is a constant process of God's self-realization in the world according to Hegel.

12 TMS II.iii.3.2.

An Economic Dimension of the Kingdom of God

The other point to be mentioned is about an economic dimension of the kingdom of God. We generally believe that the kingdom of God is a theological issue irrelevant of economics. However, many biblical images of the kingdom of God has a strong undertones of an economic dimension; for example, 'no one who has left home or wife or brothers or parents or children for the sake of the kingdom of God will fail to receive many times as much in this age and, in the age to come, eternal life' (Luke 18:16–30). It is reasonable to assume that the saying would be understood by the disciples and others surrounding him as an investment for the future when he says that there is a reward to receive a hundred times as much. Then, could we say that Jesus is an economist advising a future-oriented investment at the sacrifice of the present life in his explanation of the kingdom of God?

Jesus' explanation of the kingdom of God has not only a theological aspect but also an economic dimension. He is surely an economist, but his approach to an economic benefit based on self-interest essentially has a theological aspect. He is also a theologian, but his approach to the kingdom of God fundamentally has an economic dimension. If there is any problem for us to properly understand the passage, it is not his but ours, as we believe that economics and theology have little in common. Self-denial, self-sacrifice, or others-interest is not different from self-interest. They are two different faces of human self-consciousness.

This economic dimension of the kingdom of God may be also recognized in Adam Smith's story about the poor man's son in his *The Theory of Moral Sentiments*.[13] The main concern of the poor man's son in heaven is an economic one. This is a good example to show that our theological concern for the last things cannot free us from self-interest. In the story, taking into account that the expression of the kingdom of God is not used in his works, we need to pay close attention to the fact that the eschatological desire for happiness of the poor man's son in heaven is an extension of his desire for economic wealth on earth. This economic approach to heaven is neither wrong nor strange. We cannot deny that there is self-conscious desire even in human self-sacrifice or others-interest.

13 TMS IV.I.8.

Therefore, the kingdom of God is not just a theological issue, but it is essentially an economic one. An afterlife or a life to come that has a strongly religious and theological undertone is fundamentally economic. It might seem to be peculiar in the mind of a rational human baptised by modern economic rationality. However, ironically, it is true that the wealthier the society we live in is, the more we seem to yearn for salvation like the wealthy man in the biblical story. We have hope for a life to come as we have a natural fear of death and an innate desire for happiness. Therefore, eschatology is not just theological, but it is economic as well in the theology of economics. The maximization of satisfaction could be the most important target not just in economics but also in theology.

8.4. Summary and Conclusion

The theological dimension of self-conscious desire is the link connecting economic desire with eschatological faith in the theology of economics of Adam Smith and Hegel. This conclusion comes from analyzing the selective and limited passages that embrace theological clues that might be related to their economic ideas. Eschatology is not just a theological issue but an economic one as well, for human self-conscious desire is at the centre of our concern for the last things in the theology of economics. Eternality is an important issue to both of them. However, from Hegel's perspective, it is the matter of the present, while it is about the world to come in Adam Smith's thought. This bifurcation comes from their different theologies. God's self-realization in the world is the foundation of Hegel's eschatology, and God's never failing goodness is the base of Adam Smith's. In spite of their different ideas of God, both have no apocalyptic tension in their eschatology. Hegel's eschatology is present-oriented hope, while Adam Smith's is future-orientated heaven. Self-conscious desire is the strongest motive in their approaches to eternality.

CHAPTER 9

Economics and Theology of Salvation in Adam Smith and Hegel

There are many different meanings of salvation such as material affluence, eternal life, authentic existence, relationship, deification, and righteousness, to name a few. What is salvation for Adam Smith and Hegel? How do they believe it is possible to reach it? Is it here and now in this world or there and then in a world to come, or both? That is the question of this chapter. By showing that self-interest is neither secular reason nor the consequence of the Fall but God's providence, and that salvation has three dimensions, it will conclude that Adam Smith's salvation is individual, other-worldly, and to be given by God, while Hegel's salvation is communal, this-worldly, and to be realized with God.

9.1. Self-interest, the Fall, and Salvation

Augustine's prayer of confession is probably one of the best examples showing an intense aspiration for salvation. He says in the beginning of his *Confessions* that 'he desires to praise thee, this man who is only a small part of thy creation. Thou hast prompted him, that he should delight to praise thee, for thou hast made us for thyself and restless is our heart until it comes to rest in thee.'[1]

1 Augustine, *Confessions and Enchiridion* (Outler: SCM Press, 1955), 400.

Interestingly, his confession that we are born with the constant desire for salvation that never stops until we are satisfied by true relationship with God is resonant with Adam Smith's saying that the desire of bettering our condition comes with us from the womb and stays until we die. He says that 'the principle which prompts to save is the desire of bettering our condition, a desire which, though generally calm and dispassionate, comes with us from the womb, and never leaves us till we go into the grave.'[2]

Then the question is: is there any fundamental difference between the constant desire of bettering one's condition as the foundation of Adam Smith's economics and the endless desire for resting in God as the essence of Augustine's theology? Both desires are seemingly different to each other in the sense that the latter is desire for God, and the latter is desire for the self. They are however the same in the sense Augustine and Adam Smith believe that the endless human desire comes from the womb and never stops until we die. The endless desire is expressed as the strongest motive for salvation in Augustine and self-interest in Adam Smith. When Augustine starts his *Confessions* from the desire for salvation, Adam Smith begins his works from the desire for self-interest. Then the question to be followed is: is Adam Smith a secular human without any concern about salvation? Is Augustine a religious human who is not interested in self-interest? Is Adam Smith's desire for self interest nothing but a secular and worldly reason that is devoid of religious faith? Is Augustine's desire for God a sacred and spiritual faith that is free from self-interest? In those questions, there is a fundamental tension between human reason and religious faith as a way of salvation. Faith seeking understanding is the famous phrase of Anselm who tries to harmonize them. As discussed in the previous chapters, this desire is natural weakness of humanity for Adam Smith and rational (*vernunftig*) power for Hegel. The tension between natural weakness and rational power as a way of salvation is succinctly expressed in Harrison's conclusion of his book. He argues that the origin of modern science including economics is not from an awareness of the power of human reason but from a conscious-

2 WN II.iii.28.

ness of fallen humanity.[3] Theological consideration is of vital importance in his understanding of the way of salvation.

I agree with his argument that human reason needs to pay attention to theological faith to explore a way of human salvation from the Fall. However, the question is: whose theology? Different theology provides different analysis of human behaviour. His theological position regarding the meaning and role of the Fall in human salvation leads him to argue that the present age is the interval between the Fall and the end (eschaton). Secular reason is then between the fallen nature and the new creation in his theology.[4] Therefore, he regards Adam Smith's thought based on self-interest as one of many examples showing that fallen humanity is naturalized in the secular world.[5]

In this book, it is argued that nature is one of two main poles that support self-interest in Adam Smith's theology of economics. Thus, I agree with Harrison's argument that self-interest is naturalized in Adam Smith's theology of economics. However, God's providence, the other pole, is not taken into account in his approach to self-interest. In Adam Smith's theology, as discussed in chapter 7 about theodicy, self-interest is not a necessary evil, nor a fortunate flaw of humanity. It is rather a gracious gift from God in Adam Smith's theology as self-interest is human nature given by God's providence. Adam Smith's self-interest cannot be an example of the triumph of secular reason over theological faith. It is rather an example of the theological faith embedded in secular reason as self-interest is a providential gift by God whose goodness never fails in the secular world or in the world to come in his theology of economics. Self-interest is not evil to be overcome but to be celebrated as God's grace.

3 Peter Harrison, *The Fall of Man and the Foundations of Science* (New York: Cambridge University Press, 2007), 258.

4 Ibid.

5 Ibid., 255.

9.2. A Triadic Approach to Salvation

A triadic approach to salvation may help to clarify the points regarding how economics and theology are interrelated, and how their relationship contributes to understanding the role of self-interest for salvation. Interestingly, three different levels of desire for salvation are embedded in the Lord's Prayer: daily bread at an economic level, forgiveness at a moral level, and deliverance at a theological level. We may note that it is composed of three different kinds of desire, which may be reminiscent of the three dimensions of self-conscious desire discussed in the chapters 2 and 3.

Firstly, salvation has an economic dimension. The prayer for daily bread shows that the economic dimension of self-interest is one of the foundations of the relationship between God and humankind. The first request in the prayer is to ask God to 'give us today our daily bread'. Asking for daily bread is related to an economic dimension of human self-conscious desire. Daily bread is certainly an economic matter of life and death as no one can survive without food in this physical world; hence, it is not trivial but rather very pertinent to pray for food as a condition to be satisfied for an economic salvation from hunger. We are human beings to be saved in body as we live in this physical world.

Indeed, we live in the society which seems to have been born again by an economic baptism. We cannot think of salvation separately from economic matters just as we cannot survive without daily bread. Therefore, the first request in the Lord's prayer is understandably about an economic issue. We are constantly conscious of the necessity of salvation from economic hardships. The human relationship with God has an economic dimension. From the first request in the Lord's Prayer, we may conclude that salvation has an economic dimension, and self-interest is the central motive for economic salvation.

Secondly, salvation has a moral dimension. The second request in the Lord's Prayer is to ask God to 'forgive us our sins as we forgive those who sin against us'. Asking for forgiveness is related to a moral dimension of the human relationship with God. We are required to ask God to forgive us our sin as we also forgive those who sin against us. The second request in the Lord's Prayer gives an idea of how to understand the moral dimension of the human self-conscious desire for salvation in relation to God and humans. We are required to pray for God's forgiveness as we are in a moral relationship with God. However, the Lord's Prayer teaches us to forgive those who sin against us so that we would be forgiven our sins because we are in essence moral beings in relationship with others. Unless we first forgive those who sin against us, we are not yet ready to receive forgiveness from God. From the second prayer, we may conclude that self-interest has a moral dimension as we all have the self-conscious desire for moral salvation from ethical depravity. Self-interest is at the centre of the human self-conscious desire for a moral salvation.

Thirdly, salvation has a theological dimension. The essence of the Lord's prayer is in its theological dimension of the human self-conscious desire for salvation. Humans are religious beings that have a self-conscious desire for theological salvation from sin and evil. The prayer for deliverance shows that the theological dimension of self-interest is one of the foundations of the relationship between God and humans. The third desire mentioned in the Lord's Prayer is to ask for God 'not to lead us into temptation but to deliver from evil'. It shows us that self-interest has a theological dimension as we all have the self-conscious desire for religious salvation from evil and sin. Self-interest is at the centre of the human self-conscious desire for religious salvation.

As briefly shown from the three aspects of salvation in the Lord's Prayer above, we may recognize quite a different tone from those that generally regard self-interest as the consequence of fallen humanity. In the Lord's Prayer, self-interest is at the centre of human self-conscious desire for economic, moral, and religious salvation. A question is then how to achieve salvation? Adam Smith would say that self-interest is at the centre of the human self-conscious desire for economic salvation in the market.[6]

Raphael (2007) argues that economics and ethics are separate areas in Adam Smith's works, so it is a crude interpretation to analyze ethical behaviour based on sympathy and benevolence from an economic perspective based on self-interest. He says:

6 WN.I.ii.2.

> Nobody but a beggar depends chiefly on benevolence and even the beggar does not depend on it entirely. *That implies that we do all depend on benevolence to some extent.* The main point of the passage, to be sure, is that we would be foolish to count on benevolence for most of what we want: we should in general expect people to think of their self-interest. *Nevertheless the passage does not warrant an assumption that all action is self-interested* (italics mine).[7]

However, the point is not whether all action is self-interested as probably assumed by economists but certainly denied by Raphael, but whether self-interest is the strongest motive of human behaviour. In my opinion, Adam Smith would say that self-interest is the strongest desire in human behaviour not only in the market but also in moral relationships and religious faith because it has economic, moral, and theological dimensions, as discussed so far. Self-interest as natural desire given by God's providence is not in conflict with sympathy and benevolence as self-interest has moral and theological dimensions. Self-interest is neither secular reason nor the consequence of the Fall, but God's providence in Adam Smith's theology of economics. If a moral dimension of self-interest is missed in economists' approach to Adam Smith's thought as Raphael argues, then a theological dimension of self-interest is overlooked in his ethical approach to Adam Smith's thought. We may notice the absence of the theological dimension of self-interest in his argument that 'Adam Smith does not regard ethics as dependent on theology and so there was no need for him to include any discussion of theology in his book on the theory of ethics.'[8] His conclusion is that Adam Smith's belief changes from an orthodox Christian theism in the original version of *The Theory of Moral Sentiments* to a non-Christian theism in the later version.

Then the question is: which theology and whose theology? As Harrison (2007) argues, theological consideration is of vital importance in the foundation of science in general, and in Adam Smith's economic ideas in particular. However, in my opinion, Adam Smith's self-interest is not

7 D.D. Raphael, *The impartial spectator: Adam Smith's moral philosophy* (Oxford: Clarendon, 2007), 115–116.

8 Ibid., 94–95.

related to the Fall, but to the goodness of God in Adam Smith's theology of economics. Self-interest is not the secular reason that denies its origin from theological faith, but the theological faith embedded in the seemingly secular reason because it is natural desire given by God's providence. Therefore, self-interest as natural instinct given by God's providence is a way of salvation in Adam Smith's theology of economics. We need to pay close attention to his theology of economics in which economic ideas and theological thought are not divided but united through the theological aspect of self-interest.

9.3. Salvation in Adam Smith and Hegel

The language of salvation itself has a religious flavour, so it will be helpful to start from the Bible to see how it is defined or used in various contexts, for Hegel also believes that he clarifies Christian theology. We are finite beings in time and space for we cannot be everywhere at the same time although Hegel believes that we become finite-infinite through the development of self-consciousness. Is salvation a matter of the present or future? Is salvation here in this world or in the world to come? Interestingly, we can find in the Bible many verses using the past, present, and future tense; for example, salvation was given in hope (Romans 8:24); salvation has come to the tax collector's house (Luke 19:9); salvation will be given to the human who stands firm to the end (Matthew 10:22). In addition, the kingdom of God has come (Luke 11:20); the kingdom of God is near (Mark 1:15; Luke 21:31); the kingdom of God is within us, not here or there (Luke 17:21). These various appearances of salvation depend on how we understand God, humans, and the world.

In fact, the expression of salvation is not used at all in Adam Smith's main works including *The Wealth of Nations* and *The Theory of Moral Sentiments*, neither is it used in Hegel's *Philosophy of Right* except several cases depending on translation. One clear usage of Hegel's use of the expression of salvation is shown in his description of the religious salvation as *the hope of eternal salvation of the individual* when he deals with morality as mediation between abstract right and ethical life.[9] In his argument, the hope of eternal salvation of the individual is contrasted with his idea: *the realization of this-worldly salvation of the community*. There are several reasons why it is so.

Firstly, he seems to try to clarify his own meaning of salvation by putting religious salvation in the context of morality. Morality for him is the focal point in the difference between antiquity and the modern age, but it is an individual conscience, a subjective freedom in Hegel's language, to be transcended and preserved in his ethics. By doing so, we may assume, he prepares to argue that salvation is not *of individual morality* (*Moralität*) but *of communal ethics* (*Sittlichkeit*). Secondly, he puts the religious salvation of the individual in the same category with love and the romantic, so he seems to contrast religious salvation with a real salvation which is the rational in his thought. If so, his argument will be that salvation is not of individual feeling but of communal rationality. Thirdly, eternal salvation is used as a negative implication to clarify his idea of salvation from the religious one classified in the same category with love and the romantic. By this clarification, he seems to assume that religious salvation is an emotional hope for an imaginary eternality. However, in Hegel's thought, the real salvation is not *other-worldly* but *this-worldly*.

In short, in Hegel's thought, religious salvation as the hope of eternal salvation of the individual is classified into the same category as love and romance. According to him, this emotional, individual, and other-worldly salvation, which is classified in the same category with love and romance, needs to be developed into rational, communal, and this-worldly ethics for a real salvation because morality and evil have the same common root in self-certainty.[10] Hegel's approach to salvation is rational, communal, and this-worldly.

9 PR 124.
10 PR 139.

Then, what should we do to achieve salvation? For example, should we sell everything we have and give it to the poor? Will there be then treasure in heaven? (Mark 10: 17–22)

It would be not only the man of the Bible, who is disappointed with the answer, for it seems to be neither easy nor possible for us to give up all our wealth without hesitation regardless how much we have, and be separated from our family and society to have salvation in this world or in the world to come. This is the reason why Hegel would not be happy with the answer. Hegel argues that the question itself put to Jesus is on the right track for salvation, as universal good is realized only by doing the right things to promote not only the welfare of our own but the welfare of others as well. However, Hegel believes that salvation is neither emotional abstraction out of the rational reality nor individual separation from the community.

The disciples are even more amazed to hear how hard it is for the rich to enter the kingdom of God, so their question is, 'Who then can be saved?' The answer is, 'With man this is impossible, but not with God; all things are possible with God' (Mark 10:27). Suddenly, the focal point of the communication changes into a new dimension: from an economic wealth to a theological faith; from impossibility to possibility; from human achievement to God's action. In the conversation, the one-dimensional perspective of salvation fixed on economic wealth is transcended and preserved in the horizon of the kingdom of God, for the main point is not in what we can do but in what God will do. Therefore, as shown in the previous section's triadic approach to salvation in the Lord's Prayer, salvation is a matter of the relationship of the self, others, and God.

In Hegel, salvation is the matter of the universal good to be realized by doing the right thing for the well-being of all. Salvation is a universal good to be achieved by the development of individual self-consciousness through which God is to be realized in the world in Hegel's thoughts. There are three main points in Hegel's arguments regarding salvation: firstly, salvation is to be achieved by the development of individual *self-consciousness*; secondly, salvation is to be achieved by the development of individual self-consciousness with *God's realization*; thirdly, salvation is to be achieved by the development of individual self-consciousness with God's realization *in the world*. In short, self-consciousness is a way of salvation to be achieved by the self-conscious rationality of individuals with God's self-realization in the world. In contrast, Adam Smith believes that salvation is a gift to given in the world to come by God whose goodness never fails in this world and in the world to come.

Comparison Between Adam Smith's Salvation and Hegel's Salvation

Adam Smith's Salvation	Hegel's Salvation
• Individual Salvation	• Communal salvation
• In a world to come	• In this world
• Salvation by natural self-interest	• Salvation by rational self-consciousness
• Salvation to be given	• Salvation to be achieved
• Afterlife	• No Afterlife
• Kingdom of God in completion	• Kingdom of God in process
• Love as sympathy	• Love as recognition
• Evil as self-negligence not scarcity	• Evil as natural instinct and poverty
• Providence through invisible hand	• Providence through cunning of reason
• God transcendent over the world	• God immanent in the world
• God is always good and perfect	• God to be realized in the state
• Natural happiness	• Rational happiness
• Eternality of individual	• Eternality of the world
• Salvation in the future	• Salvation in the present

Individual Salvation and Communal Salvation

If salvation is to be saved from economic, moral, or theological evil, then a question we may think of is whether it is individual or communal. Hegel argues that salvation is to be achieved in this world rather than in a life to come as the state is the march of God in the world.[11] In Hegel, salvation cannot be separate from economic justice in the world since God is to be realized in the world. The rational self-consciousness cannot be realized unless there is economic justice in the world. That is the reason the ethical state is required to be the essential moment of the ethical life in the world

11 PR 258 Addition.

where God is to be realized. Salvation is the universal good *to be achieved in the world* by development of individual self-consciousness in the ethical state which is the march of God who is to be realized through the self-autonomy of individuals. In Hegel, salvation is in essence social freedom; freedom cannot be achieved without the development of self-consciousness transcending the laws of nature.

However, this story is the complete opposite to the case of Adam Smith who believes that the ultimate salvation is not in this world but in a life to come. By theological faith in a transcendent God, he is able to be freed from the shackle of our duty to achieve universal good in the world, for our salvation is not necessarily contingent on the economic and ethical life. This theological difference between them is the pivotal point to understand the difference of the economic and moral ideas between Hegel and Adam Smith. In Adam Smith's God, God is transcendent; however, God never fails in his goodness, so we are never God-forsaken in this world. The proof of God being with us in his never-failing goodness is an inherent desire of self-interest by the wisdom of Nature in Adam Smith's thoughts. By this, Adam Smith connects human self-interest with God's transcendence through the nature of wisdom. Adam Smith accepts human weakness as natural; however, he believes that human weakness is the grace of God who never fails to take care of the world. Therefore, we may conclude that, according to Adam Smith, true salvation is not something to be achieved in the world by the development of self-consciousness as in Hegel's thought, but something *to be achieved in a life to come individually*. Of course, Adam Smith argues that our effort for happiness in this world is important not only for ourselves but also for others, for he believes that the great Author will render to everyone to the works he performed in this world.[12]

In addition, the point of Adam Smith's argument is that salvation is open to everyone regardless of whether one is poor or rich, or whether the civil society has in itself ethical defects or not. Adam Smith would say that what is not possible with human is possible with God for salvation is in essence in a life to come; however, Hegel would say that what is not

12 TMS III 5.10.

possible with humans is not possible with God either, since salvation is essentially in this world. In Adam Smith, we are individually free in our desire of searching for self-interest; however, true happiness is only in a life to come.

Consequently, in Hegel's thought, we cannot be free unless we are social as our consciousness is something to be realized in relation to others, for salvation is in essence communally realized in the world. However, in Adam Smith's thought, we cannot be social unless we are free as self-interest is something to be given individually, for salvation is in essence personally received rather than communally realized. Different theology leads to different economics.

Salvation as Grace and Salvation as Achievement

Is salvation a human achievement by our effort or God's gift we may receive freely? Hegel argues that human salvation is related to God's realization in the world rather than something to be given by a transcendent God as in Adam Smith. For Smith, however, this world is neither real nor rational, but transient and natural. Salvation is therefore possible only in the world to come rather than in this world. God is not such a self-actualizing reason in this world through human self-consciousness as in Hegel; rather, God is the transcendent Creator who is good in essence in spite of invisibility in reality. God is, for Smith, good but invisible rather than rational but cunning as in Hegel. Humans are weak but not left alone. God is invisible but works through the invisible hand.

Adam Smith believes that self-interest is a way of salvation for individuals and society as it is to be given as providential nature in humankind by the goodness of the transcendent God. Adam Smith would say that salvation is not something to be achieved in the present world by God's self-realization in the world through our rational self-consciousness; rather it is to be given by God's providence through our natural self-interest in the world to come. Human weakness is not something to be done away with rational reason. Let God be God and humans be humans. Hegel's salvation is basically philosophical when he says that true philosophy leads to

God while a half-philosophy leads away from God. He mentions God as the telos which a true philosophy leads to. True philosophy for him leads to human salvation. It is important to note that Adam Smith's salvation is essentially economic when he says that an invisible hand makes almost the same distribution of the necessities of life for the real happiness of human life.

Adam Smith's Happiness and Hegel's Happiness

Although the expression of salvation is never used in Adam Smith's main works, and hardly used in Hegel's *Philosophy of Right*, the word happiness is frequently used in both of them. By understanding their different approaches to happiness, we may be able to clarify the nature of salvation in Adam Smith and Hegel's works. According to Hegel, happiness is something we have to achieve in the world through the development of self-consciousness. The mediation between humans and their happiness is the state without which humans cannot be free.[13]

Then, it is reasonable to conclude that Hegel's approach to happiness or welfare is something to be achieved in the state. Hegel's happiness should be here and now rather than in the future, because there is no eternality except in this world in his theology of economics. If happiness is real, then it is rational (*vernunftig*) in Hegel's thought. True happiness is in rational self-realization in the world, so regarding the present as vain and looking beyond it is nothing but irrational and therefore unreal.

In contrast, however, happiness is something to be given equally to all according to Adam Smith, as human happiness is the wisdom of God.[14] According to him, we can still be happy here and now even though he believes that this world is full of vanity, and his idea of eternality is future-oriented.[15] The possibility of happiness here and now is emphasized again

13 PR 126, PR 265 Addition.

14 TMS II.ii.3.5.

15 TMS IV.I.10.

in his story about the poor man's son.[16] True happiness is not in vanity but in ease and tranquillity, which is available here and now because this world is presided over by God's providential goodness that never fails. In this transient world, according to him, happiness is natural but easily overlooked by human weakness.

From the perspective of the theological foundations embedded in Adam Smith's economic ideas, we may conclude that happiness is a state of mind. Humans can be happy as they are, regardless of their circumstances. He believes that even beggars can be happy here and now regardless of their economic situations, as God's goodness never fails. Therefore, according to his theology of economics, happiness is not an achievement to be gained by human effort, but a discovery and awareness to be found.

For Hegel, the human desire for happiness is a matter of reality to be achieved here and now in this world, while for Adam Smith it is a matter of vanity in this world but to be finally given in a world to come. Hegel believes that humans may achieve self-realization by rational self-consciousness in this world where God himself is to be self-actualized in the state. However, Adam Smith believes that true happiness is not possible in this world as we have an endless desire of bettering one's condition, which is finally satisfied only in the world to come. This difference between them is related to their theology of economics. For Hegel, God is immanent in this world, self-actualizing in the state, so we can and should realize our happiness here and now in this world by the development of rational self-consciousness. Natural instinct is an evil against happiness which is to be realized. For Adam Smith, God is transcendent over the world, so true happiness is postponed until we are in the world to come. Hegel's happiness is to delight in the present, so he says: 'here is the rose, dance here'. Adam Smith's happiness is not in the transient vanity of material wealth in this world but in ease and tranquillity, a humble expectation of the life to come. In his thoughts, this world of constant desire is a vanity. Neither Adam Smith nor Hegel believes that happiness is in economic wealth.

16 TMS.IV.1.8.

Adam Smith's happiness and Hegel's happiness are different to each other. Adam Smith's thought, happiness is calmness, peace and happiness, while, for Hegel, it is self-actualization. For Hegel, happiness in the world is absolute as this world is the place where God's self-actualization is achieved. For Adam Smith, happiness in the world is conditional as this world is transitive and there is a world to come where true happiness is possible. For Hegel, happiness is to recognize reason as the rose in the cross of the present, and to find delight in it. Happiness is rational insight which implies reconciliation with reality. Happiness is not a good feeling without or beyond the reality of this world, but a rational recognition of the reality of the world. Happiness is natural for Adam Smith, and rational (*vernunftig*) for Hegel. Rational self-consciousness is a way to happiness in Hegel's thought, while natural self-interest is a way to happiness in Adam Smith's. Adam Smith would say that we are able to be happy now as it is natural. Hegel also may say the same thing as it is rational. We are unhappy because humans are, in Adam Smith's theology of economic life, easily deceived by the human self-conscious desire, and because humans are, in Hegel's theology of economic life, in need of self-realization.

There are many different kinds of theologies, emphasizing various aspects of salvation: for example, liberation theology, existential theology, secular theology, evangelical theology, to name a few. If salvation is a matter of rightness before God, Adam Smith would say that we have a triadic relationship with God as we have self-interest in human nature as a gift, which is economic, moral, and theological. Human nature is the gateway to the right relationship with God in his theology of economics. Hegel would also say that the human self-realization as the dialectical development of self-consciousness is rightness before God. If salvation is a matter of a human relationship with God, Adam Smith would say that we were, are and will be in relationship with God as self-interest as the desire of bettering one's condition is the natural instinct. He believes that it was given as a gift by God's providence, and is not left alone but guided by the invisible hand, and will be turned into real peace and tranquillity in the world to come. Hegel also would say that we are in a relationship with God as we have the self-consciousness to be realized by God's providential self-realization in the state. If salvation is a matter of human deification as assumed by some early church fathers, Adam Smith would say that human beings are different from God as the former is weak and the latter is all-knowing, all-powerful, and the ultimate wisdom. And he believes that the weakness is not a curse but blessing as God's goodness never fails in this world and in the world to come. There is a qualitative difference between God and humans in his theology of economics. Hegel however would say that humans become God as God is to be realized in the world through human self-realization in the state. There is no boundary between God and humans in his theology of economics. If salvation is a matter of authentic human existence as in existential theology, Adam Smith would say that self-interest is the gateway to authentic existence as it is essentially based on faith in God rather than just on the transient material world. Hegel also would say that self-realization is the only way to authentic human existence. If salvation is a matter of liberation as in liberation theology, Adam Smith would say that natural self-interest as a gift from God is the way to liberation. Hegel also would say that rational self-consciousness leads us to freedom and liberation.

9.4. Summary and Conclusion

In conclusion, in Hegel's theology of economics, we cannot be free, happy, or saved unless individuality is united with communality by self-realization in the state where God is to be realized. That is a true happiness and salvation in his thought. However, in Adam Smith's theology of economics, we can be free and happy individuals just as we are, regardless of whether we be a king or a beggar, as long as self-interest is in union with God's wisdom without falling into transient vanity.

Furthermore, even in our vanity, Adam Smith believes that self-interest works for others-interest. Smith believes that this world is not eternal, so salvation is not here in this transitory world, but in the world to come. Thus, Adam Smith's salvation is basically other-worldly, but Hegel's salvation is essentially this-worldly. Salvation is not fully experienced in this transitory world, but will be found in full in the real world to come in Adam Smith's theology of economic life. In Hegel's theology of economic life, salvation is to be fully recognized in this eternal world as long as we have reason (*vernunft*). Adam Smith's salvation is individual compared to Hegel's salvation that is communal. This difference does not necessarily mean that they neglect either individual salvation or communal salvation respectively. Rather, it shows that theological precepts affect their economic approaches. In Hegel, there is no individual salvation as such, unless there is no communal salvation. Adam Smith however believes that there is no communal salvation without individual salvation. The human self-conscious desire is natural self-interest of individuals for Adam Smith, and rational (*vernunftig*) self-consciousness of community for Hegel. Therefore, salvation is a matter of grace in Adam Smith's perspective, and a matter of achievement in Hegel's. For both of them, salvation is a matter of being with God, but God is more immanent in this world for Hegel, compared to Adam Smith who believes that God is transcendent over the world.

Smith was raised in a Calvinist context and Hegel in a Lutheran one. Their historical and religious backgrounds might affect their theology and economic ideas. The main concern of this book is however neither to clarify whether Smith or Hegel is a Calvinist or a Lutheran in their respective religious backgrounds, nor to evaluate the merits or demerits of those influences, but to describe the links that might be hidden or embedded in their theology of economics.

CHAPTER 10

Conclusion: Dialogue Between Economics and Theology to Be Continued

10.1. Summary

Despite economics and theology being generally believed to have little in common, they are interrelated in the theologies of economic life of Adam Smith and Hegel. The relationship can be explained in two ways. One is that economics is theology. Economics is not an instrumental science merely allocating scarce material to its best uses without any purpose or direction, but is founded on theological precepts that are embedded in economic thoughts. The other is that theology is economics. Theology is not a theoretical discipline simply searching for a spiritual truth devoid of economic reality, but is based on the human relationship with God, of which self-interested consciousness is the central motive. Theological faith is not irrelevant to economic reality. The theologies of economic life in Adam Smith and Hegel are examples from which we may recognize the inter-relationship.

At the centre of the mutual relationship of economics and theology, there is a theological dimension of self-interest. We cannot separate one from the other without truncating the essential elements of each. In the theology of economics of Adam Smith and Hegel, self-interested consciousness is founded on theological precepts beyond scientific investigation: a providential gift by God's grace for Adam Smith, and a rational power in God's self-realization for Hegel. Human self-conscious desire as the foundation of modern economics is a theological faith rather than a scientific truth. Without theological foundations, economics would be nothing but one-dimensional, calculative, and instrumental rationality devoid of any teleological direction. In addition, theological thought is fundamentally economic as it is closely related to the self-conscious desire that is the strongest motive in economics. Without taking the human self-conscious desire into theological thought, we cannot properly understand the meaning of the religious human behaviour that theology tries to explain. The mutual relationship is more than just an ethical matter.

Self-conscious desire is not moral depravity or religious sin but a way of salvation, for it is a providential gift for Adam Smith and a rational power for Hegel. The desire of searching for one's own interest is a human nature with various colours. It has a much broader connotation than the narrowly presumed notions such as economic rationality, moral selfishness, and religious sinfulness. As self-conscious beings, we are all concerned about our own salvation. Self-interest is the primary motivation of human activity in all areas including economic, moral, and even religious circles. Be it commercial trade, virtuous morality, or religious faith, we cannot deny that self-conscious desire for bettering one's condition is one of the strongest desires of ordinary people. It is a way of salvation. Thus, God-love could be another name of self-love, and vice versa. Theology and economics are not mutually exclusive but inter-related to each other.

Adam Smith's sympathy and Hegel's recognition are two different models describing the same human relationship based on self-interested consciousness. Self-interest and others-interest does not contradict each other anymore. Rather, they are two sides of the same self-consciousness. The tension is overcome by God's providence in human nature for Adam Smith, and God's providence in human reason for Hegel. The process is synthetic for the former as he believes that nature is good, but dialectical for the latter as he believes that nature is something to be overcome by reason. This difference comes from their different theological assumptions. The theological concept of Original sin has a central role in Hegel's theology of economics, while the never-failing goodness of God is the base of Adam Smith's.

Those theological and anthropological assumptions are embedded in the problematic but meaningful expressions such as Adam Smith's invisible hand and Hegel's cunning of reason. The invisible hand is the providence of an all-powerful God whose goodness never fails even in human weakness, while the cunning of reason is the providence of a self-negating God who is to be realized in the world through human self-realization. Adam Smith's invisible hand is logical and consistent in his works when it is approached from the theological dimension of self-interest that is indispensable in his theology of economics. The invisible hand is a pertinent term expressing his theological perspective that God is transcendent over the world as a person whose goodness and benevolence never fails both in this world and in the world to come. Likewise, the cunning of reason is a necessary concept to convey his theological standpoint that God is to be realized as a self-negating entity in this world full of passion.

Economic poverty in the world is an evil to be overcome in Hegel's theology of economic life as it leads to ethical depravity. The individual passion based on self-interest in the market needs to be elevated and rationalized in the state that is the rational organization where God is to be realized in the world. In contrast, Adam Smith believes that this world is fundamentally perfect, being created by God the Creator who is all-powerful, all-knowing, and always good. Poverty is not an evil in his theology of economics. We can still be happy without wealth in the world created by God. The point is that humans are different from God as we are weak and fragile. Human weakness is not something to be negated as in Hegel, but to be celebrated as a grace of God in his theology. This human weakness is not an obstacle but a vantage point. It becomes a motive for accumulation of economic wealth. However, it needs to be emphasized that the desire for wealth is the result of human weakness, not the result of the human power of reason. This means that Adam Smith does not believe that salvation or happiness is not from economic wealth. This economic world is transitory and transient in his theology. His theological backgrounds are more fundamental than generally assumed in modern economics, ethics, and theology. Adam Smith is a theologian who does not neglect the other-worldly element of human existence nor deny the this-worldly factor of human salvation.

Accordingly, material scarcity is not an evil for Adam Smith, while it is an evil to be overcome as long as it leads to ethical depravity according to Hegel. This world is full of God's goodness, so we can naturally be happy here and now even though we are beggars in his theology. For Hegel, however, we live in the world where God is to be realized by self-negation, so we can rationally be happy here and now but in the state, the ultimate community where God is to be realized. Therefore, it is natural for Adam Smith to have faith in an after-life in his eschatology. This world is transitory and humans are weak, so eternal life cannot belong to this world, but in a world to come where true peace and calmness are in his eschatology. However, according to Hegel, this world is eternal as God is to be realized in this world, so his eschatology is present-oriented with faith in the rational ability of humans.

A relationship between transcendence and immanence is a theological issue regarding the way of God's existence. Smith's God is in a sense an immanent divinity as Smith believes that God's goodness never fails in the world. We could also say that Hegel's God is a transcendent divinity as he believes that God is not exactly the same as the world according to his panentheistic understanding of God. However, Smith's God is strongly transcendent compared to Hegel's understanding of God because Smith's God is self-sufficient apart from the world, while Hegel's God is mostly immanent compared to Smith's understanding of God because Hegel's God is not a self-sufficient being apart from the world.

Consequently, salvation is other-worldly, individual, something to be given in Adam Smith's theology of economics, while it is this-worldly, communal, and something to be achieved in Hegel's. In spite of their differences of thought, Smith and Hegel's works have a similarity in the sense that economic thought and religious faith are intertwined in their economics of theology. In addition, they are complementary to each other in our understanding the role of human desire because self-interest and self-negation are two different faces of the same self-centred consciousness of humans, even though Smith puts more emphasis on self-affirmation than self-negation compared to Hegel.

10.2. Contributions

The central aim of this interdisciplinary research is in showing that economics and theology are mutually intertwined, and that understanding the inter-relationship contributes to a better understanding of human behaviour not only in world of economics but also in the ethical and religious world including salvation. The main points are the theological dimension of self-interest, the intertwinement of economics and theology, and the clarification of the meaning of salvation.

It is argued that human self-conscious desire has a theological dimension. This conclusion may open many ways towards a meaningful dialogue between economics and theology as it gives a clue towards overcoming the present dichotomy between modern economics and theology. The theological dimension of self-interest may be used as a bridge for communication between economics and theology as this book has clarified the theological nature of economic rationality on which modern economics is founded. It has also shown that the nature of self-conscious desire is both natural and rational, based on the theologies of economics of Adam Smith and Hegel.

Developing the theological role of self-interest, it is also clarified that the relationship between economics and theology is more than just a matter of ethics, so we need to pay close attention not only to the theological aspect of economic behaviour but also to the economic dimension of theological faith. This means that different theology may lead to different economics, and that different economic ideas could be the result of different theological backgrounds. Then, we may ask an important question: what kinds of theological ideas are embedded in modern economics? What kinds of economic ideas are implanted in modern theology? The mutual relationship between economics and theology may help to explore possible answers to this significant question.

Finally, based on the inter-relationship between economics and theology, I have clarified the meaning of salvation by showing that salvation has economic, moral, and theological aspects. The clarification of the role of God's providence in human self-conscious desire enriches our understanding of salvation. Material scarcity is not necessarily evil, but probably God's providence for human weakness in the theologies of economic life of Adam Smith and Hegel. In this sense, the invisible hand and the cunning of reason are not awkward, ironic or inconsistent expressions, but are God's providence embedded in the theological dimension of self-interest in the thoughts of Adam Smith and Hegel respectively. Consequently, economic scarcity as God's providence for human weakness may harmonize the seemingly conflicting approaches to salvation between economic rationality and theological faith. Salvation is not to be properly understood without taking into account the providential aspect of self-interest and the inter-relationship between economics and theology.

10.3. Limits

There are however some limits to this book. Firstly, the conclusions are mainly from the comparison of two particular thinkers: Adam Smith and G.W.F. Hegel. Secondly, the book is limited to the area where it is possible to compare them, so it is not a full account of the thoughts of both Adam Smith and Hegel. Thirdly, there is a gap between Adam Smith's political economy and modern economics, so a conclusion deduced from the analysis of Adam Smith's theology of economics cannot be generalized to modern economics. Finally, the concept of salvation chosen as the contact point in this book is not the only contact point between economics and theology. Other contact points such as competition, for example, could lead to different conclusions. Despite these limits, I hope this interdisciplinary research contributes to a better understanding of the mutual relationship between economics and theology so as to properly understand human behaviour not only in the world of economics but also in the ethical and religious world.

References

Alvey, J.E. 'A Short History of Economics as a Moral Science.' *Journal of Markets and Morality* 2/1 (1999): 53–73.

——. 'The Hidden Theology of Adam Smith: A Belated Reply to Hill.' *European Journal for the History of Economic Thought* 11/4 (2004): 623–628.

Anderson, G.M. 'Mr Smith and the Preachers: The Economics of Religion in the Wealth of Nations.' *Journal of Political Economy* 96 (1988): 1066–1088.

Anderson, J. and G. Langelett. 'Economics and the Evangelical Mind.' *Bulletin of the Association of Christian Economists USA* 28 (Fall 1996): 5–24.

Augustine. *Confessions and Enchiridion*. London: SCM Press, 1955.

Azzi, C. and R.G. Ehrenberg. 'Household Allocation of Time and Church Attendance.' *Journal of Political Economy* 83/1 (1975): 27–56.

Barrera, A. *God and the Evil of Scarcity: Moral Foundations of Economic Agency*. Notre Dame, IN: University of Notre Dame Press, 2005.

Barth, K. and E. Brunner. *Natural Theology: Comprising 'Nature and Grace' and 'No!'* London: Geoffrey Bles, 1946.

Becker, G.S. *Human Capital: A Theoretical and Empirical Analysis, with Special Reference to Education*. New York; Columbia University Press, 1964.

——. *The Economic Approach to Human Behavior*. Chicago, IL: University of Chicago Press, 1976.

Becker, G.S. *Human Capital: A Theoretical and Empirical Analysis, with Special Reference to Education*. Chicago, IL: The University of Chicago Press, 1993.

——. 'Nobel Lecture: The Economic Way of Looking at Human Behaviour.' *Journal of Political Economy* 101/3 (1993): 385–409.

Beed, C. and C. Beed. 'A Christian Perspective on Economics.' *Journal of Economic Methodology* 3/1 (1996): 91–112.

——. 'The autonomy of economics from Judeo-Christian thought: a critique.' *International Journal of Social Economics* 30/9 (2003): 942–966.

Brams, S. *Biblical Games: A Strategic Analysis of Stories in the Old Testament*. Cambridge: MIT Press, 1980.

——. *Superior Beings: If They Exist, How Would We Know?* New York: Springer-Verlag, 1983.

Brennan, Geoffrey. The Impact of Theological Dispositions on Economics: A Commentary. *Economics and Religion: Are They Distinct?* Boston, MA: Kluwer, 1994.

Britton, A. 'Introducing Religion into Economic Theory.' *Journal of the UK Association of Christian Economists* 32 (2003): 27–36.

Britton, A. and P. Sedgwick. *Economic Theory and Christian Belief.* Bern: Peter Lang, 2003.

Bruce, S. 'Religion and Rational Choice.' *Sociology of Religion* 54 (1993): 193–205.

Davis, J.B. 'Smith's Invisible Hand and Hegel's Cunning of Reason.' *International Journal of Social Economics* 16/6 (1989): 50–66.

Durlauf, S.N. and L. Blume. *The New Palgrave Dictionary of Economics*. New York: Palgrave Macmillan, 2008.

Ekelund, R.B.J., R.F. Hebert, et al. 'An Economic Model of the Medieval Church: Usury as a Form of Rent Seeking.' *Journal of Law, Economics and Organization* 5/2 (1989): 307–331.

Fleischacker, S. *A third Concept of Liberty: Judgment and Freedom in Kant and Adam Smith*. Princeton, NJ: Princeton University Press, 1999.

——. *On Adam Smith's Wealth of nations: A philosophical companion*. Princeton, NJ: Princeton University Press, 2004.

Foley, D.K. *Adam's Fallacy: A guide to Economic Theology.* Cambridge: Harvard University Press, 2006.

Frey, D.E. 'The Good Samaritan as bad economist: Self-interest in economics and theology.' *Cross Currents* 46/3 (1996): 293–302.

Grampp, W.D. 'What Did Smith Mean by the Invisible Hand?' *Journal of Political Economy* 108/3 (2000): 441–465.

Grenz, S. and R.E. Olson. *20th-century Theology: God and the World in a Transitional Age.* Downers Grove: Inter Varsity Press, 1992.

Halteman, J. 'Is Adam Smith's Moral Philosophy an Adequate Foundation for a Market Economy?' *Markets and Morality* 6/2 (2003): 453–478.

Harrison, P. *The Fall of Man and the Foundations of Science.* New York: Cambridge University Press, 2007.

Hegel, G.W.F. *Early Theological Writings*. Chicago, IL: University of Chicago Press, 1948.

——. *Elements of the Philosophy of Right*. New York: Cambridge University Press, 1991.

——. *Hegel's Science of Logic.* Atlantic Highlands: Humanities Press International, 1989.

——. *Lectures on the Philosophy of Religion: One-volume Edition: the Lectures of 1827*. Berkeley, CA: University of California Press, 1988.

——. *Phenomenology of Spirit.* Oxford: Clarendon Press, 1977.

——. *The Philosophy of History*. New York: Dover, 1956.

Heyne, P. 'Passing Judgements.' *Bulletin of the Association of Christian Economists USA* 23 (Spring 1994): 9–15.

Hill, L. 'Further reflections on the "Hidden Theology" of Adam Smith.' *European Journal for the History of Economic Thought* 11/4 (2004): 629–635.

——. 'The Hidden Theology of Adam Smith.' *European Journal for the History of Economic Thought* 8/1 (2001): 1–29.

Hirschman, A.O. *The Passions and the Interests: Political Arguments for Capitalism before Its Triumph.* Princeton, NJ: Princeton University Press, 1977.

Hodgson, P.C. *Hegel and Christian Theology: A Reading of the Lectures on the Philosophy of Religion.* Oxford: Oxford University Press, 2005.

Hollis, M. *The Cunning of Reason*. Cambridge: Cambridge University Press, 1987.

Honneth, A. 'Recognition and Moral Obligation.' *Social Research* 64/1 (1997): 16–35.

Iannaccone, L. 'Introduction to the Economics of Religion.' *Journal of Economic Literature* 36/3 (1998): 1465–1495.

——. 'Sacrifice and Stigma: Reducing Free-Riding in Cults, Communes, and Other Collectives.' *Journal of Political Economy* 100/2 (1992): 271–291.

——. Rational Choice: A Framework for the Scientific Study of Religion. *Rational Choice Theory and Religion*. New York: Routledge, 1997.

Inwood, M.J. *A Hegel dictionary*. Oxford: Blackwell, 1992.

Keynes, J.M. *Essays in Persuasion*. London: Macmillan, 1931.

Kleer, R.A. 'Final Causes in Adam Smith's Theory of Moral Sentiments.' *Journal of the History of Philosophy* 32/2 (1995): 275–330.

——. 'The Role of Teleology in Adam Smith's Wealth of Nations.' *History of Economics Review* 31 (2000): 14–29.

Knight, F.H. 'Ethics and Economic Reform: Christianity.' *Economica* 6 (November 1939): 398–422.

Leathers, C.G. and J.P. Raines 'Adam Smith on Competitive Religious Markets.' *History of Political Economy* 24/2 (1992): 499–513.

Long, B. 'Adam Smith's Natural Theology of Society.' *Adam Smith Review 2* (2006).

Long, D.S. *Divine Economy: Theology and the Market*. London: Routledge, 2000.

Long, D.S., N.R. Fox, et al. *Calculated Futures: Theology, Ethics, and Economics*. Waco: Baylor University Press, 2007.

Macfie, A. 'The Invisible Hand of Jupiter.' *Journal of the History of Ideas* 32 (1971): 595–599.

MacIntyre, A. *After Virtue – A Study in Moral Theory*. London: Duckworth, 1981.

——. *Whose Justice? Which Rationality?* London: Duckworth, 1988.
Mandeville, B. *The Fable of the Bees or Private Vices, Publick Benefits*. Indianapolis: Liberty Classics, 1988. Edited by F.B. Kaye. (Oxford: Clarendon Press, 1924; repint, Liberty Fund, 1988. Part 1 is from the 6th edition, 1732).
McCleary, R.M. 'Salvation, Damnation, and Economic Incentive.' *Journal of Contemporary Religion* (October 2006).
McCleary, R.M. and Barro, R.J. 'Religion and Economy.' *Journal of Economic Perspectives* 20/2 (2006): 49–72.
McCloskey, D.N. *The Bourgeois Virtues: Ethics for an Age of Commerce*. Chicago, IL: University of Chicago Press, 2006.
McGrath, A.E. *The Christian Theology Reader*. Oxford: Basil Blackwell, 1995.
——. *Christian Theology: An Introduction*. Malden: Blackwell, 2002.
Meeks, D. *God the Economist: The Doctrine of God in Political Economy*. Minneapolis, MN: Fortress Pres, 1989.
Milbank, J. *Theology and Social Theory: Beyond Secular Reason*. Oxford: Basil Blackwell, 1990.
——. *Theology and Social Theory: Beyond Secular Reason*. 2nd ed. Malden: Blackwell, 2006.
Montgomery, J.D. 'Contemplations on the Economic Approach to Religious Behaviour.' *American Economic Review* 86/2 (1996): 443–447.
Myers, M.L. *The Soul of Modern Economic Man: Ideas of Self-Interest, Thomas Hobbes to Adam Smith*. Chicago, IL: University of Chicago Press, 1983.
Nelson, R.H. 'Economic Religion versus Christian Values.' *Journal of Markets and Morality* 1/2 (1998): 142–157.
——. *Economics as Religion: from Samuelson to Chicago and Beyond*. USA: Pennsylvania State University Press, 2001.
——. 'The Theological Meaning of Economics.' *Christian Century* (August 1993): 777–781.
——. *Reaching for Heaven on Earth – The Theological Meaning of Economics.* Savage, MD: Rowan and Littlefield, 1991.
Novak, M. *The Spirit of Democratic Capitalism*. New York: Simon and Schuster, 1982.
Oslington, P. 'Adam Smith as Theologian.' Unpublished work in progress. Templeton Advanced Research Workshop 2009.
——. 'A Rational Choice Model of Divine Action.' *Journal of the UK Association of Christian Economists* 35 (2005): 25–32.
——. 'A Theological Economics.' *International Journal of Social Economics* 27/1 (2000): 32–44.

——. 'Divine Action, Providence and Adam Smith's Invisible Hand.' Unpublished work in progress. ANU seminar August 2008.

——., Ed. *Economics and Religion*. International Library of Critical Writings in Economics. 2 volumes. Cheltenham: Edward Elgar, 2003.

Pannenberg, W. *Jesus – God and Man*. London: S.C.M. Press, 1968.

——. *Theology and the Philosophy of Science*. Philadelphia, PE: Westminster Press, 1973.

Pinnock, C.H. *Tracking the Maze: Finding Our Way Through Modern Theology from an Evangelical Perspective*. San Francisco, CA: Harper & Row, 1990.

Plant, R. *Hegel*. London: Allen and Unwin, 1973.

——. 'Hegel and Political Economy – II.' *New Left Review* 104 (July 1977): 103–113.

——. 'Hegel and Political Economy – I.' *New Left Review* 103 May (1977): 79–92.

Raphael, D.D. *The impartial Spectator: Adam Smith's Moral Philosophy*. Oxford: Clarendon, 2007.

Richardson, J.D. 'What Should Christian Economists Do? ...Economics!' *Bulletin of the Association of Christian Economists USA* 23 (Spring 1994): 12–15.

Rothschild, E. 'Adam Smith and the Invisible Hand.' *American Economic Review* 84/2 (May 1994): 319–22.

——. *Economic Sentiments: Adam Smith, Condorcet and the Enlightenment*. Harvard, CA: Harvard University Press, 2001.

Schweiker, W. and C. Matthewes, eds. *Having: Property and Possession in Religious and Social Life*. Grand Rapids, MI: Eerdmans, 2004.

Smith, A. (1776). *An Inquiry into the Nature and Causes of the Wealth of Nations*. Oxford: Oxford University Press, 1976. Edited by R.H. Campbell, A.S. Skinner and W.B. Todd.

——. (1795). *Essays on Philosophical Subjects*. Oxford: Oxford University Press, 1980. Edited by W.P.D. Wightman and J.C. Bryce.

——. (1759). *The Theory of Moral Sentiments*. Oxford: Oxford University Press, 1975. Edited by D.D. Raphael and A.L. Macfie.

Smith, I. 'A Rational Choice Model of the Book of Revelation.' *Journal for the Study of the New Testament* 85 (2002): 97–116.

——. 'Modelling Faith.' *Journal of the UK Association of Christian Economists* 34 (2004): 1–15.

Taylor, C. *Hegel*. Cambridge: Cambridge University Press, 1975.

——. *Hegel and modern society*. Cambridge: Cambridge University Press, 1979.

Tiemstra, J.P. 'What Should Christian Economists Do? Doing Economics, But Differently.' *Bulletin of the Association of Christian Economists USA* 23(Spring 1994): 3–8.

Torrance, T.F. *Reality and scientific theology*. Edinburgh, Scottish Academic Press, 1985.

Ullmann-Margalit 'The invisible Hand and the Cunning of Reason.' *Social Research* 64 (Summer 1997): 182–198.

Viner, J. 'Adam Smith and Laissez Faire.' *Journal of Political Economy* 35 (April 1927): 198–232.

——. 'Religious Thought and Economic Society.' *History of Political Economy* 10/1 (1978): 9–189.

——. *The Role of Providence in the Social Order*. Philadelphia, PE: American Philosophical Society, 1972.

Vivenza, G. *Adam Smith and the classics: the Classical Heritage in Adams Smith's Thought*. Oxford: Oxford University Press, 2001.

Walsh, V.C. *Scarcity and Evil*. Englewood Cliffs, NJ: Prentice-Hall, 1961.

Waterman, A.M.C. 'Economics as Theology: Adam Smith's Wealth of Nations.' *Southern Economic Journal* 68/4 (2002): 907–921.

——. 'Is "Political Economy" really a Christian Heresy?' *Faith and Economics* (Spring 2008).

——., Ed. *Political Economy and Christian Theology Since the Enlightenment: Essays in Intellectual History*. London: Palgrave Macmillan. 2004.

——. *Revolution, Economics and Religion: Christian political economy, 1798–1833*. Cambridge: Cambridge University Press, 1991.

——. *The Beginning of Boundaries: The Sudden Separation of Economics from Christian Theology*. Edited by G. Erreygers. *Economics and Interdisciplinary Research*. London: Routledge, 2001.

Williams, R. *Hegel's Ethics of Recognition*. Berkeley, CA: University of California Press, 1997.

Wogaman, J.P. *Economics and Ethics: A Christian Enquiry*. London: SCM, 1986.

Index